"Once again in this book, as he has done in numerous activities as a teacher, Mr. Shefter displays marked ability to pinpoint difficulties and to devise clever, effective methods of meeting them. Readers will profit from the rich talents and broad teaching experience of the author."

JAMES V. TAGUE

Principal, Port Richmond High School, N. Y.

"Mr. Shefter introduced a course in spelling in this division. The results indicated that the instruction had been exceedingly effective. I am happy to hear that he has decided to make his program of study available to the general public through this book."

PROFESSOR WARREN BOWER, ASSISTANT DEAN

Division of General Education, N. Y. U.

". . . Thank you for making elementary education fascinating entertainment. I shall never forget how to spell 'supersede, cemetery, all right'."

From one of many enthusiastic letters written by Mr. Shefter's television students.

SIX MINUTES A DAY
TO
PERFECT SPELLING

by

HARRY SHEFTER

FOREWORD BY PAUL A. McGHEE
Dean of the Division of General Education
New York University

POCKET BOOKS, INC. • NEW YORK, N. Y.

This original edition, prepared especially for Pocket Books, Inc., is printed from brand-new plates made from newly set, clear, easy-to-read type.

Six Minutes a Day to Perfect Spelling

CARDINAL edition published September, 1954
1st printing .... July, 1954

*To Evelyn
and our two little ladies—
Barbara and Sharon Ann*

Table of Contents

Foreword

"Harry Shefter is one of the best teachers of English to cross my path. Whether in prep school, high school, in our program of special classes for adults at New York University—where he introduced the first course to be offered on spelling—or over television, to a spelling 'class' of 2,000 registered students, Harry Shefter teaches with zest and wit and freshness of attack on old problems. As a contributor of articles to educational journals he has specialized in unique methods of instruction. His article 'The Subway Speller,' appearing in a monthly University publication, and given wide publicity in New York newspapers, mentions self-teaching ideas incorporated in the present book. Those who buy this book will come in contact with an extraordinarily stimulating and helpful teacher."

PAUL A. MCGHEE
Dean of General Education
New York University

SIX MINUTES A DAY
TO
PERFECT SPELLING

Good Spellers Are Made,
Not Born!

Please write your name in pencil below:

Ronald Miller

You just wrote your name.

When was the last time you misspelled it? You probably can't remember. Spelling your name is automatic. You do it without thought, without hesitation, knowing it will come out right. *There is no reason, then, why you can't do the same with any word in the English language.*

I'm going to show you how. That's *my* job. I will also tell you how to practice, so that correct spelling can stay with you forever. That will be *your* job. We'll work as a team, and sooner than you dare expect, you will be able to spell any word you want as easily and automatically as you do your name. This is not an idle promise. I have seen it come true time and time again with students in my classrooms.

Why does a person always spell his own name correctly? The reason is simply that he has made the words in his name a part of him. He has reduced their spelling to the habit level. Mind you; this is as true of Aleksandra Trzettizorriskaya (a student of mine some years ago) as it is of John Brown, Jack Smith, or you.

It stands to reason then that your spelling will improve when you learn to treat other words the same way. Reduce them to the habit level. Make them a part of you.

Don't worry about long nights of study devoted to impossible-to-remember rules and procedures. This is not that kind of book. All you will need is SIX MINUTES A DAY of your time. All you will have to learn is five simple steps:

SEE THE WORD!

THINK THE WORD!

FEEL THE WORD!

SAY THE WORD!

BUILD THE WORD!

That's all: Six minutes a day and five steps.

Let's begin by clearing away some bad spelling alibis. A popular one is that weakness in spelling runs in families. Grandpa had lots of trouble, Papa used to chew the pencil to bits when he wrote, and naturally

Junior can't be expected to do any better. Nonsense! Each slipped into the same bad habit, and not one of them bothered to break it.

Perhaps someone has said to you:

"How can I ever learn to spell? The sounds in the language don't seem to agree with the letters. I write *ENOUGH*. The *GH* sounds like an *F*. Then I find that in *PHONE* the *PH* is also an *F* sound. When I get to *OFTEN*, the *F* is an *F* but the *T* is nothing!"

This kind of poor speller blames our language for his troubles. There are too many silent letters, he says; too many peculiar combinations that don't spell the way they sound.

He seems to have a point. Consider how the English language grew. The ancient history of the British Isles is the record of one invasion after another. About three thousand years ago, the first invaders, variously known as Celts, Gaels, or Britons, made their appearance in Scotland, Ireland, Wales, and England. Although these tribes stayed over nine hundred years, they left little evidence of their language. Less than one percent of the contents of a modern unabridged dictionary can be traced to these earliest inhabitants.

About 55 B.C., Caesar's legions started to bully their way into England. Strangely, however, the strong Latin and Greek influence on English did not occur in the four hundred years of Roman occupation, but came during the revival of learning in the Renaissance period and from eighteenth century classical scholars like Dr. Samuel Johnson.

After the Romans, Teutonic hordes—Angles, Saxons, and Jutes—came storming in. By 500 A.D. the remnants of the original Britons had been driven to obscure regions, and Anglo-Saxon became the foundation of the language we use. Words such as WISDOM, BEGGAR, WEAKLING, and OWNERSHIP, while containing some unclear vowel sounds and doubled consonants, would not have presented very serious problems.

However, in 1066, William the Conqueror's Frenchmen surged across the Channel and began to force new words into the language. BAILIFF, MORTGAGE, EMBELLISH, CHAMOIS, CAMOUFLAGE, and TECHNIQUE are typical words of French ancestry that contain silent letters which baffle poor spellers.

A few centuries later, the delayed Roman influence set in. Examples like AQUARIUM, ASTERISK, ACHIEVEMENT, STATISTICIAN, and CHIROPRACTOR show the kind of "jaw-breakers," as some call them, that began to appear in English. Often mere length of a word or unusual letter combinations are enough to floor the timid. "Looks too tough!" we say.

Even after the thirteen colonies had become the United States, and had adopted the language of their forefathers, borrowing went on freely. We reached into the Scandinavian countries and took RANSACK, DAHLIA, FLOUNDER, and SLEIGH among others. MACARONI, MOTTO, DILETTANTE, and COLONNADE are but a few of the words Italy gave us.

From Spain we appropriated BARBECUE, BRONCHO, LARIAT, SOMBRERO, and others. Hebrew, Arabic, Indian, Persian, Slavic, American Indian, African, and Chinese are additional languages that enriched our vocabulary, but added to our spelling problems.

Is it any wonder that English has no pattern? We take foreign words with complicated letter formations, don't bother to simplify them, and dump them right into the hopper. Then off we go on another merry spelling jamboree, or so it seems.

But if this were the basic cause of our troubles, we would just throw up our hands and hope for the best. Actually, scientific studies prove that through the years *most spelling mistakes are made with simple, everyday words.*

The classic collection of frequently misspelled words, found in every grade school speller and called "The Hundred Spelling Demons," is a good example. Take a look at this list at the beginning of the Appendix (pages 181 and 183). Not one of the demons looks frightening, does it? Yet these words, and others like them, give poor spellers most of their headaches.

Poor spelling is, therefore, neither inherited nor completely created by the structure of the language. How DOES it come about? Almost always, the trouble starts early in life AND BECOMES A BAD HABIT.

To be analytical for a moment, here are the stories of real people who let themselves fall into misspelling traps. Each is typical of how a poor speller is made, not born.

The Case of Mr. A.

He was introduced to the mystery of the written word by a rather grim-faced school teacher. The weekly spelling tests became moments of sheer horror. Poor marks increased his sense of failure. After a while, he unconsciously began to resist the whole annoying business. He fought back by deliberately showing that he didn't care. A certain amount of attention came his way because of his difficulty.

To live up to his reputation young A. developed misspelling into a habit. Today, although he is a reasonably successful salesman, he frequently finds himself embarrassed by his problems with words.

The Case of Mr. D.

He left school early to open a small store selling automobile accessories. Last year the fourth branch in a modestly-growing chain was introduced. This intelligent, rising business man is an official in the local Kiwanis, has become prominent in church affairs, and two weeks ago was invited to join a committee to draft a new city charter. Since this is the first time his writing and speaking abilities will come under the public eye, he's worried. Up to now, mispronunciations and misspellings have never been too important. Miss Corbett, his secretary, has been discreet about notes that came to her attention from his desk. She quietly revised errors like "probly, fillum, usialy"—all caused by incorrect pronunciations. Now, however, Mr. D. risks open exposure of his slovenly speech and writing. Accurate spelling and proper pronunciation go hand in hand, AND ONE DOES WASH THE OTHER. Our disturbed friend will have to decline the invitation. Until he has improved his verbal skills, he'll have to keep his weaknesses to himself.

The Case of Miss B.

She is a junior executive in an advertising agency. Everyone predicts a bright future for her. Although her record in college was brilliant, she constantly had trouble with the English courses. The instructors complained that they could not read her work because of her terrible handwriting. And carelessness in this respect led her to sloppy spelling habits. She would become confused when asked whether a particular letter should be "i" or "e," "a" or "o." Now a question that haunts her is: "Will my spelling weakness eventually cost me my job?"

The Case of Mrs. C.

This lady takes great pride in her sparkling new home in the suburbs. Since she likes to entertain and take part in club activities, she often finds it necessary to send notes and letters. But she dreads the task because it becomes a major undertaking. An hour or so with the dictionary and a floor littered with discarded sheets of stationery have become the symbols of this ordeal. Mrs. C. has just never learned to *see* a word with her *mind* as well as with her eyes. She needs to be trained to visualize so that the letters will not form a filmy blur, and spelling will not become an emotional catastrophe.

The Case of Mary E.

She is suffering from a serious brain injury. Talking and writing are very trying experiences. She sees words as you would if you held a paper up to a mirror. Often the letters become jumbled. Only her doctor, through his medical skill and knowledge, can be of any real assistance to her.

There they are. Each is an exhibit in a gallery of poor spellers. One has lost his confidence; another can't say the word right, much less spell it; the third let her slipshod penmanship get her into trouble; the fourth hasn't learned to get a mental picture of the word. Yes, there are good reasons why they can't spell and good reasons why they should improve. But only Mary E. needs more than a fresh start. Everyone else can rid himself of his spelling problems by breaking bad habits and substituting good ones.

You've just reviewed the causes of poor spelling. Whatever yours are, get moving in the right direction today. There are lots of things in your favor. For instance, your personal list of "spelling demons" with which you will have to work isn't as long as you think. I dare say that, if you could remember and write down the words you always misspell, you'd come up with fewer than fifty or sixty. Secondly, you really want to do something about your spelling. Otherwise you wouldn't even be reading this. And certainly, if in a short time you can look any word squarely in the eye, it will be worth the effort you make in following the suggestions outlined here.

Let's get down to business. Let's look at the tricks of the trade.

On a piece of paper, write out calenDAR rapidly, "looking" at the picture of the word with your mind's eye all the while. Repeat the whole procedure three times.

.   .   .

Here are some other devices you can use to set up the image:

1. Try colored crayon for the difficult part, and plain ink or pencil for the rest of the letters.

2. Separate the parts, and underline the difficulty:

cal en dar

3. Circle the key part:

calen (*dar*)

4. Use the number 2 to remind you that certain words are always written in two parts:

all **2** right

Spellick #1

If you think you've never seen the word "spellick" before, you are right. It was invented for this book. **SIX MINUTES A DAY TO PERFECT SPELLING** is a complete course in itself. The only additional tools you need are a dictionary, a pencil and some paper, things you should already own. There are, however, some other very useful tools which you can build for yourself . . . if you have the time and, more important, if you have the desire to get ahead as fast as possible. We have called these extra devices *spellicks*, the gimmicks or special tricks in this business of learning to spell. *Spellicks* are separated from the rest of the instruction because they are extras rather than musts. But *spellicks* are the *power tools* of spelling. Use them if you possibly can. Here is *spellick* number one:

Cut a piece of *yellow* cardboard about two feet long and about six inches wide. Use this as the background. Cut other pieces of cardboard of the same color into strips about a foot long and three inches wide. On one such strip print, in *black letters*, the word you are studying at the moment. As you print, make the letters of the difficult part twice the size of the others. Now you have an excellent tool for SEEING THE WORD. The black on yellow will greatly sharpen the image. Just lean the background card against a solid object like a book end, and place the word card in front of it.

Of course, you continue the process of staring at the image for ten seconds, looking away, counting five, trying to create a mind picture, and then writing the word out rapidly as you visualize it.

SEE THE WORD with these:

arGUMent	ILLiterate	quaRRel
barGAIN	judGMent	reCOMMEND
sePARate	keroSENE	SECRETary
DEStroy	leISure	tempERAture
enVELope	manAGE	UNable
femiNINE	neCESSary	VINEgar
grATEful	oCCasion	wHISTle
handKERchief	PARTner	

Review Paragraph

As a review of this chapter, we have prepared a paragraph containing every key word mentioned in the explanatory material. Naturally, the real test of your ability to spell correctly is in your own writing when you are not deliberately being careful. Therefore, we have used the paragraph form, rather than a list, to make the situation as natural as possible.

These essays are not offered as literary gems. The need to keep them short and at the same time have them contain a special group of particular words creates a problem. Nevertheless, the occasional near-nonsense sentence should not interfere with your main objective, which is to use these paragraphs as a test of how much you have learned!

The best method of course is to ask someone to read aloud to you as you write. If you must work on the material by yourself, simply rewrite it. Look at the key words (those words in boldface) *only long enough to identify them*, not long enough to help you spell them. See the difficult part of each word *in your mind*, not in the text as you get to it in the sentence. Use the blank spaces below the paragraph to jot down the words you missed. Study these again!

If you wish to study a typical **feminine argument**, I **recommend** that you visit a **bargain** counter. You will see how two shoppers can sometimes **manage** to get into a **quarrel** over even a **handkerchief**. In the **judgment** of each unwilling **partner**, she simply must have the article for her **leisure** moments. On one **occasion** I saw the **temperature** of a **secretary** go up as if it were lighted **kerosene**. She had picked up a **calendar** in an **envelope**, but a bystander had been **unable** to resist reaching for it, too. One would have thought both were **illiterate** from the looks washed in **vinegar** that passed between them. Each surely would have been **grateful** if she had been able to **destroy** the other. It looked for a moment as if a **whistle** would have to be blown to **separate** the pair, but a **saleslady** made everything **all right** when she pointed out that the item was not even for sale.

illiterate destroy all right
feminine argument management
grateful (separate) vinegar
manage saleslady whistle

judgement necessary kerosene

envelope handkerchief bargain

temperature secretary unable

occasion leisure quarrel recommend

I will continue the practice of giving you a summary paragraph at the end of each chapter that deals with a special skill. Your score should be 100% before you are satisfied. For example, in the foregoing paragraph if you got only 23 of the 24 key words right you should eliminate your error before going ahead.

A word or two about tests in general, and spelling tests in particular. In most areas of information, it is customary to use an examination to measure general knowledge in the field. In school subjects, for example, the traditional 65% or higher indicates satisfactory achievement. Similarly, a mark of 85% might be excellent on a state professional or civil service examination.

But such grades in a spelling test would be meaningless! They would indicate only the percentage of words that need further study. The speller cannot be satisfied with 85% or 90% or 98%. He must strive for 100% EVERY TIME.

You will not, therefore, find any tests here designed merely to allow you to get a score. All the sentences and paragraphs at the ends of chapters or in the appendix are there to help you learn two things:

> the words you still have to study,

> the words you have already mastered.

Toying with long lists of deliberately-misspelled examples of errors or picking out the correct forms from several possibilities is an utter waste of time. In fact, it is dangerous to concentrate your attention on the *wrong* spelling at any time. Your mind may not choose to remember the right one the next time you have to use the word! For this reason, there are no distorted spellings or useless tests in this book.

SEE THE WORD,

now . . .

Think the Word!

Look very quickly at each of the ten words listed below. In the space provided write the first thing that pops into your mind. Try to make your response as automatic as you can.

AUNT _uncle_   FEAR _ful_

BLUE _green_   GIRL _friend_

CARE _package_   HEAD _ache_

DUTY _bound_   IRON _hard_

EASE _go_   JUNE _july_

Now examine each combination, the original word and the one you inserted. What made AUNT suggest

uncle to you? Think about it for a moment. If you wrote the name of a person in the space, isn't she the one you like best, or possibly never could tolerate? If you wrote SAD after BLUE, isn't it that the color depresses you for one reason or another? If you put CHAIR or COUCH after EASE, you probably identify relaxation with a favorite piece of furniture. But no matter what you wrote down, by filling in the spaces, you participated in what psychologists call an "association of ideas."

16

This term applies to a very basic human characteristic. The faculty of your mind that helps you remember things is constantly establishing these BONDS. It explains why the strains of a familiar bit of music can bring back a picture of a wonderful evening you once spent; why you'll reject a certain kind of food because it makes you think, perhaps subconsciously, of those harrowing mornings you spent on the high chair struggling with your persistent mother; why the number 16 may mean a dreamy birthday party to a girl.

In the ability of your mind to associate lies the key to another secret of good spelling. You have learned how to get a mental picture of the difficult part of a word. Now if you can place a mental string around your finger in addition to the image in your mind, the result will be startling. When you tie in the problem syllable with an instantly-recalled idea, you will have another strong aid toward the proper spelling of a word. The secret is simply to form a BOND.

Let's go back to CALENDAR, the example we used to point out how advisable it is to *see* the word with the *mind* as well as the *eye*. The A between the D and R is the trouble-maker. Now invent a statement that creates a BOND between the difficult part and an easily-remembered idea. For example: According to the calenDAR, the D. A. R. will meet this week. There it is. The abbreviation of the name of the famous feminine group reminds you of the A between the D and R. It can even be an entertaining game. The rules are simple:

1. Set up the association.

2. Make it as silly or unusual as you can. Oddly enough, one tends to remember nonsense more readily than logic.

3. Try to combine this association with an image in your mind as explained in the previous chapter. See the word AND think the word! Thus you make the difficult part of the word both the basis for the IMAGE and the association for the **BOND**.

4. Once you've decided on a good combination, study it for ten seconds, look away toward another surface, SEE AND THINK the problem syllable, and then write the whole word out rapidly.

Take a look at these additional examples. After you have become thoroughly familiar with the method, gradually make up a list of your own.

1. It is VILE to allow special priVILEge.
2. The suit on the SERGEANT looked like SERGE on an ANT.
3. She screamed, "EEE!" as she passed the cEmEtEry.
4. The VILLAIN enjoyed his VILLA IN the hills.
5. Scientists LABOR in a LABORatory.
6. GM (General Motors) sent an acknowledGMent.
7. Every AGE has its trAGEdy.
8. You GAIN when you buy a barGAIN.
9. My PROF is called PROFessor Gordon.
10. He lost his TEMPER AT the rise in TEMPERATure.
11. Don't MAR your writing with bad gramMAR.
12. Draw ALL the lines parALLel.
13. There was constant rePETition of his PET phrase.
14. TEN times later his persisTENce was rewarded.

15. She flew into a RAGE at his outRAGEous remarks.

16. EMMA was in a dilEMMA.

17. When I think of FeBRuary, I say, "BR!"

18. It was an ERA of great litERAture.

19. The princiPAL is my PAL.

20. You RILE me with your sacRILEgious remarks.

21. StationERy is for a lettER.

22. When he ATE, he was grATEful.

23. "ACH!" There goes the parACHute.

24. My skin shows resisTANce to TAN.

25. He would sooner DIE than be obeDIEnt.

It may occur to you at this point that some of the BONDS don't seem to help you very much. This is as it should be. The bonds must be made up BY YOU! You will remember what YOU have created far better than something thought of by another person.

Here again is the summary paragraph. Try it after you have mastered the foregoing group of words. Remember: it is better if this material is dictated to you.

Review Paragraph

Early in February an acknowledgment written on official stationery came from the laboratory. By this time the police chief's temperature was at the boiling point. The tragedy of the torn parachute, discovered by the persistence of Sergeant Bristol, remained unsolved. The villain was still at large, and there wasn't even a principal suspect. But the chief had faced a dilemma before. In grammar which a professor would never use and a minister might call **sacrilegious** he ordered his men to search every part of the city, even the **cemetery**, and to break down the **resistance** of anyone brought in. The **outrageous** crime had no **parallel** in the **literature** of murder, but it is the **privilege** of a seldom **grateful** public to demand results. Police chiefs are **obedient** to a public mood, and in this case the public, fearing a **repetition** of the crime, was in no mood to **bargain**.

February acknowledgment temperature stationery tragedy parachute

---

Spellick #2

If you have no one available to dictate these paragraphs, there is still a way to solve the problem. Try to borrow a recording machine. Perhaps a friend has one. Then you can simply record the material in this and other chapters. Thereafter, you can play back the paragraphs at your leisure, and write as you listen. You will find the page numbers of all the summary paragraphs in the index for quick reference.

There are many advantages to such an arrangement. The fact that you hear YOUR OWN VOICE dictating should help you remember. You can play the tape or record as often as you like, stop whenever you please, and even make up essays of your own for further tests. If you use this suggestion, be careful to observe these cautions for the actual recording:

1. Speak clearly into the microphone; pronounce extra-carefully. Do not leave out any syllables or letters.

2. Break up the sentences into phrases. For example:

   "Early in February — an acknowledgment — written on official stationery — came from the laboratory —"

3. Read slowly; pause long enough after each phrase to allow yourself time to write it. You can accustom yourself to the proper timing by practicing writing sentences as you read them aloud. When you think you have the tempo set, and you begin to record, ALLOW A FEW MORE SECONDS AT EACH BREAK.

4. Identify each paragraph at the beginning of the recording. Say something like: "This is the paragraph on page —." You may want to check a word or sentence at a future date, and fail to remember the source. It would be wise to repeat this information on the label, if you've used a disc, or on the outside of the container, if you did the job on tape.

5. If you aren't satisfied with a particular recording, DO IT OVER. Unless you feel comfortable as you listen, the recorded material will be more of a hindrance than a help!

So far you have learned to SEE THE WORD in your mind and THINK THE WORD by association. Now let's turn to the third important method of solving your spelling problems.

· IV ·

Feel the Word!

Have you ever watched a blind person become familiar with a strange object? He goes over the outline of the figure carefully and slowly. *Through his fingers* he is memorizing the shape. When he feels something similar again, his sense of touch will immediately identify it. In fact, this is the way a blind person learns to read Braille. But all of us have the ability to "think" and "see" with our fingers. Here are two illustrations.

You sit in a darkened movie theater. As you watch the film, you hear clicking sounds nearby. You are puzzled, but when the lights go on you discover a woman putting her knitting away. Her *fingers* have been busy in the dark while her mind was concentrating on the screen.

One morning you are late. As you dash down the steps, your fingers feverishly make a knot in your tie. Your mind, already forming excuses for tardiness, doesn't spend a second's thought on your tie. Your *fingers* are doing the thinking.

Or let me remind you about the signature you wrote on the first page. You didn't think about it. You let your *fingers* take charge. Your mind was probably wondering why you were asked to do the job.

There are many things you do almost entirely by reflex. The patterns of behavior are so habitual that your mind often operates in a secondary capacity. It has such a clear picture of the necessary movements and such a strong association with the proper reactions that the physical process becomes prompt, efficient, and almost unthinking.

You know how to SEE THE WORD. You know how to THINK THE WORD. Learn how to FEEL THE WORD and spelling will also become one of your mechanically perfect skills.

This physical attack upon words is designed to force the hand to do most of the work of spelling. It is almost the final step in enabling you to write any word as casually as you do your signature.

Try another experiment. Write the number *19836* on a blank piece of paper. Put your finger on each digit and trace it, saying it aloud as you trace. Do this three times. Turn the paper over and write the original number once more, but, as you do, say aloud *12345*. If you can write one number while saying another, you have proved that your hand can be taught to spell automatically.

This skill is particularly useful for words that contain more than one difficult part. A *bond* or *image* may not be enough to eliminate all the trouble spots.

Take the word PSYCHOLOGY, for example. A poor speller may forget that it begins with a P, or that it contains a Y and CH. It is therefore possible to make several errors. The attack must be on an over-all basis. You must *feel* the *entire* word and be able to write it mechanically.

Use this system:

1. On a piece of paper, write the word in large, well-rounded, *script* letters. About twice the size of your normal handwriting should be sufficient.

2. Place the pen or pencil you have used aside, and, WITH YOUR FINGER directly touching the letters, slowly TRACE the word, softly repeating aloud each letter as you trace it.

3. Allow no break in the rhythm. Your arm should swing along, not stopping its motion until it has completed the word. Dot the *i* or cross the *t*, if there is one.

4. Do this three times. Start carefully, and gradually increase the pace until it is very much like the speed at which you normally write.

5. After you have been able to sweep through the word confidently, without pausing, turn the paper over. THIS IS VERY IMPORTANT. SAY ANYTHING ALOUD AS YOU WRITE OUT THE WORD. Repeat your name and address, or recite a favorite bit of poetry, or simply count. You want to grasp the word in a physical sense. The hand, not the mind, must do the spelling. By talking as you write, you force yourself to make the process automatic.

6. If you make the slightest mistake, repeat the exercise until your HAND spells the word. Remember: use your finger to trace. Do not use a pen or pencil.

Here are a few more words that contain problems in several places. They can be handled best by the tracing method.

1. _minimum_

2. _campaign_

3. _ridiculous_

4. _guardian_

5. _bureau_

6. _ascertain_

7. _memorandum_

8. _mortgage_

9. _guarantee_

10. _acknowledge_

After a while, you will find that you can combine tracing with the two other techniques of seeing and thinking. Thus, if you must think about the spelling, it will help rather than hinder the writing.

Here is the easy way to combine the three steps:

1. Construct the image in your mind as suggested in the second chapter.
2. Prepare a BOND for the difficult part or parts of the word.
3. Trace the word WITH YOUR FINGER three times.
4. Write it rapidly AS YOU LOOK AT THE IMAGE IN YOUR MIND and REPEAT THE BOND ALOUD. In this way, you will be seeing the word, thinking the word, and feeling the word all at once.

If you can master this three step technique, 90% of your spelling troubles will be over.

Review Paragraph

And now the summary paragraph:

Lucy looked at Mr. Forbes, her guardian. She felt that the terms of the mortgage were ridiculous, and she clearly recalled the memorandum the head of the housing bureau had sent her. He had strongly urged some sort of guarantee of payments so that the risks would be at a minimum. She realized she would first have to ascertain what psychology would work best before she could start a campaign to force Mr. Forbes to acknowledge the justice of her claim.

SEE THE WORD!

THINK THE WORD!

FEEL THE WORD!

and . . .

Say the Word!

Here's an old time vaudeville joke, but there's more than a laugh buried in it.

A man goes into a restaurant and sits down at a table.

"I'll have some **kidley** stew," he says.

"Pardon, sir," suggests the waiter, "but don't you mean **kidney** stew?"

"I said **kidley** stew, did'l I?" replies the man.

It is very common for people to be entirely unaware of the spoken mistakes they make. These people haven't learned to listen to themselves talk. Unfortunately, oral errors are often transferred to written words. Many misspellings come directly from faulty pronunciation.

You tend to write the way you speak. Examine these:

SURPRISE   FILM

CAVALRY   JEWELRY

Say each one aloud. Try to listen to yourself as you speak. If you have trouble concentrating on your voice, use this simple device. Stand a few inches away from a wall. Hold your hands behind your ears and parallel to the wall. As you talk, you will hear the sounds as if they were coming over a microphone.

Now that you have pronounced the words, look them up in a good dictionary. You will notice that, after the spelling of a word, its proper pronunciation is indicated by certain symbols for the vowels and consonants. At the bottom of each page of text of the better dictionaries is listed the key or interpretation of these signs. Become familiar with them, but there is no need to learn the list by heart. Frequent use will fix the various marks in your memory. Also glance through the "Guide to Pronunciation" and "The Rules for Syllabication" usually found in the introductory matter. Learn how to use this information when necessary.

All right, you've checked the words. Did you leave out a syllable? Did you add one? Did you fail to say R in SURPRISE? Did you put the L before the V in CAVALRY? If you made any of these mistakes, you committed one of a number of common spoken errors that often become spelling errors.

The problem breaks down into four types of mispronunciation.

A. Extra Syllable

Some letter combinations in our language are difficult to produce orally. An M following an L is an example. The open mouth position must immediately be followed by closed lips, and stopped short. The tendency, therefore, is to add a syllable between the two letters to try to bridge the gap. Thus we get FILLUM instead of FILM.

You can train yourself to speak correctly. Slow down your speech. Give each sound its full value before producing another. If you are in doubt about a word, or you hear other people saying it differently, look it up. Practice before a mirror. Watch your lip and jaw movements. Say it right and you will spell it right!

SAY AND SPELL:

ATHLete	disasTRous	rememBRance
launDRy	hinDRance	barbaROUS
umBRella	mischieVOUS	

attacKED
E is not pronounced

drowNED
E is not pronounced

B. Omitted Syllable

It is just as wrong, of course, to leave out a syllable. Here the trouble arises out of speech that is too hurried. Slow up. Take it easy. Say the whole word. Don't say and write JOOLERY instead of JEWELRY.

SAY AND SPELL:

accidentALly	poEM	tempERature
probABly	choCOlate	labORatory

C. Incorrect and Omitted Sounds

You may occasionally use the proper number of syllables in a word, but pronounce a particular letter incorrectly or leave it out altogether. You must not be careless. Get the dictionary habit. Don't say and spell SUPPRISE when you mean SURprise.

SAY AND SPELL:

arCtic	diPHtheria	goverNment
FebRuary	sacrilEgious	quesTION

D. Reversed Sounds

Usually this error occurs as the result of hearing the word spoken incorrectly and copying the mispronunciation without bothering to check. In this way the little boy listens to his friend describe the charge of the "calvary," and may imitate this form for years before discovering that the word is CAVALRY. And imagine his dismay when he learns that there really is a word CALVARY, the hill where Christ was crucified!

SAY AND SPELL:

irrELEvant   trAGEdy

PERform   PERspiration

Right here there must be a question in your mind.

"What if I can say the word correctly, but still have trouble spelling it?"

That's fair enough. But don't forget the first three techniques. When you have removed the speech problem, treat the word like any other. SEE IT, THINK IT, FEEL IT! It's the basic attack. What we're doing now is giving you hints that can be applied to groups of words. However, the SEE-THINK-FEEL method is the guaranteed way, even if no other suggestion helps.

•   •   •

Now come additional problems related to speech.

E. The Indefinite Vowel

You know what a vowel is—a, e, i, o, u, or y (as in many and mystery). Because of the different sounds each of these can be—for example, A as in bay, bat, ball, bar, bare—the pronunciation does not always tell us what the proper letter is. This is especially true in words where the middle vowel sound is little more than a grunt. In RELATIVE, merely pronouncing the word does not clearly tell us that an A should follow the L.

Suppose, however, whenever you have to spell RELATIVE you also think of RELATE (here the A is sharply marked). Then RELATIVE becomes easy. You can use this technique with many words that fall into this class —words where the middle vowel sound is not clear, but where it *is* clear in a word from the same family.

Note these:

	Word	First Cousin
A	narrative	narrate
	sedative	sedate
	miracle	miraculous
E	arithmetic	arithmetical
	competition	compete
	celebration	celebrity
I	definite	define
	compilation	compile
	hypocrisy	hypocritical
O	frivolous	frivolity
	revolution	revolt
	consolation	console
U	exultation	exult
	sulphur	sulphuric
	future	futurity

•   •   •

You have probably had your troubles with the next group of speech–spelling puzzlers. These are words that come in pairs, or even appear as threesomes; they are pronounced exactly alike, or very nearly so, but have essential differences in meaning and spelling. You want to talk about a *stationary* object. You know that there is one word that uses an A and another that uses an E in the final syllables.

To handle these we go back to the THINK THE WORD method. Create a bond between the difficult part and some bit of nonsense. Treat each word as if it were a separate unit and you will avoid confusion.

F. Think the Words That Sound Alike!

Look at these:

1. StationAry objects stAnd still.
   StationEry is used for lEttErs.

2. A princiPAL should be a PAL.
   The principAl idea is the mAin one.
   GrapPLE a princiPLE to your heart.

3. I can't EAT in hot wEATher.
   I don't know WHETher pie will WHET my appetite.

4. A grOAN is a loud mOAN.
   When I am grOWN I shall OWN a store.

5. I hEAR with my EAR.
   We looked hERE, thERE, everywhERE.

Some words are not even pronounced alike but are close enough to be troublesome.

Watch out for:

accept-except   prophecy-prophesy

affect-effect	moral-morale
angel-angle	canvas-canvass
council-counsel	loose-lose
quiet-quite	desert-dessert

Sometimes, in an effort to be informal or conversational, a speaker or writer will use contractions. These are single words that have been made out of two. For example, IT IS becomes IT'S in the contracted form. We have, in effect, substituted an apostrophe (') for the letter I between the T and the S and made one word. Do not confuse this with ITS, the form that does not use the *apostrophe* and which indicates possession. Whenever you are in doubt about ITS or IT'S, try the sentence using the two words IT IS. If they fit, IT'S is correct; if they do not, use ITS.

Put this book in it's or its place.

Substitute IT IS. Does it make sense? It doesn't, of course. Use **its** in **its place.**

Note: There is no such form as ITS'.

This test also applies to your and you're, who's and whose, and their, there and they're.

Here are some examples:

Your or **you're** not wanted here.
(Try you are. It fits. Therefore, use **you're**.)

Your or **you're** name is John.
(Try you are. It doesn't fit. Use **your**.)

I wonder who's or whose the winner.
(Try who is. It fits. Therefore, use who's.)

I know who's or whose hat that is.
(Try who is. It doesn't fit. Use whose.)

Their or there or they're coming Sunday.
(Try they are. It fits. Therefore, use they're.)

Their or there or they're is the place we stayed last year.
(Try they are. It doesn't fit. Use there. Indicates place.)

Their or there or they're team won.
(Try they are. It doesn't fit. Use their. Indicates possession.)

Remember:

It's SHOULD'VE or SHOULD HAVE
   but never should of!

· · ·

You've tried spelling rules before. You probably gave up in disgust, too. There were so many exceptions that you finished by being more harmed than helped. That's why we're going to bother with only those rules that work so often and with so many words that exceptions are of no consequence.

This brings us to the most valuable spelling rule in the language. It, too, is tied in with pronunciation. We'll review certain speech principles first, and afterwards show how they apply in spelling to a vast number of words.

G. Accented Syllable Rule—(when to double final consonants)

Vowels—We've talked about these before: A, E, I, O, U, and sometimes Y.

Consonants—All the other letters in the alphabet. Observe that the U in EQUIP has the effect of a W. When U is pronounced W it is properly considered a consonant.

Accent—A syllable is that part of a word that is said all at once, without a break or pause in the rhythm. It might be compared to a musical note. We say the word STOP in one continuous sound, and it would be represented in music by one note. Its technical name is MONOSYLLABLE (MONO—from the Greek meaning one). POLYSYLLABLES (POLY—many) are words that contain two or more syllables or pauses. In music, we would need two notes to represent REMIT (two syllables RE-MIT) and three for PREFERENCE (three syllables PRE-FER-ENCE). When we pronounce a single-syllable word (monosyllable), we place the same amount of stress on the whole word. However, in polysyllables, only one of the syllables receives the stress. When we pronounce polysyllabic words, we use added volume or loudness on the syllable custom has dictated should receive what we call the accent.

reMIT—Added volume or loudness is placed on the second syllable.

LAbel—The first syllable receives the greater stress or accent.

PREFerence—Here again the first syllable is accented. Note, however, how there is an accent shift to the second syllable in **preFER**, even though **preference** and **prefer** are in the same word family.

Spellick #3

If you aren't sure whether you are stressing the proper syllable, even when you know from a dictionary which it should be, here is a good test. Get any flat piece of glass—a small mirror, a medicine chest shelf, or a plate. Sprinkle a little powder along the surface. Now hold the powdered piece of glass about a half inch from your lips. As you speak you'll notice that a puff of powder will be blown forward when you accent a particular syllable. Let the puff tell you whether the stress came at the right time. At first, deliberately overdo the accenting, expelling the breath with violence so that you will have no difficulty recognizing the point at which you increased the volume.

· · ·

We are now ready for the accented syllable rule, the most valuable of all spelling rules.

Observe these two groups of words:

DIF fer	oc CUR
LA bel	ad MIT
ED it	ex PEL

Similarities:

1. Each word ends in a **single consonant**.
2. Each final single **consonant** is preceded by a **single vowel**.

Major Differences:

1. In the group on the right, the accent falls on the **last syllable**.

2. In the group on the left, the accent falls on the first syllable.

Rule:

IF A WORD ENDS IN ONE CONSONANT PRECEDED BY A SINGLE VOWEL,

IF THE SYLLABLE IN WHICH THIS COMBINATION APPEARS IS ACCENTED,

DOUBLE THE FINAL CONSONANT BEFORE ADDING A SYLLABLE BEGINNING WITH A VOWEL.

•   •   •

IF THE SYLLABLE IN WHICH THE COMBINATION APPEARS IS *NOT* ACCENTED, DO *NOT* DOUBLE.

We can condense the rule into a formula:

FSA *equals* DOUBLE!

F—final single consonant
S—single vowel preceding
A—accent on the combination

Let's put the FSA rule into practice. From the groups used as examples above, take the word OCCUR. It ends in an R (single final consonant), the R is preceded by U (single vowel), and the stress falls on CUR (accent on the combination).

Therefore:

ocCUR *plus* ED (syllable beginning with a vowel) *equals* occuRRed (doubled final consonant)

OR
ocCUR *plus* ENCE *equals* occuRRence

OR

ocCUR *plus* ING *equals* occuRRing

However

Take the word DIFFER from the column on the left. There is the final consonant R, and there is the single vowel E, but the stress falls on DIF—which is NOT THE SYLLABLE CONTAINING THE COMBINATION!

Therefore:

DIFfer *plus* ED *equals* diffeRed.
DIFfer *plus* ENCE *equals* diffeRence.
DIFfer *plus* ING *equals* diffeRing.

The consonant is not doubled because the accent does not fall on the syllable containing the single final consonant preceded by a single vowel.

Here's what happens to the rest of the columns.

Last Syllable Not Accented	Last Syllable Accented
LAbel, labeLed, labeLing	adMIT, admiTTed, admiTTance
EDit, ediTed, ediTing	exPEL, expeLLed, expeLLing

In single syllable words you don't have to worry about the accent since the stress automatically falls on the entire word. All you do is decide whether there is a single final consonant preceded by a single vowel.

stop, stoPPing, stoPPed
bat, baTTing, baTTed
flat, flaTTer, flaTTen

But

meet, meeTing (two vowels precede the final consonant)

We talked about accent shifts a little while ago. Notice what happens to the word PREFER when the stress changes from one syllable to another.

preFER, prefeRRed, prefeRRing

And

PREFeRence (accent shifted to first syllable, no doubling)

Exceptions? Yes, there are some:

Double L's Instead of Single

canceLLation	crystaLLize
chanceLLor	exceLLent

French Endings

crocheTed   ricocheTed

(Note: Both words end in the AY sound, so that it is actually a vowel ending.)

Double Words

overlaPPed   outfiTTed

(Note: The first consists of OVER and Lap, has almost a double accent; therefore, this and others like it are treated as if the second half determines the spelling.)

Unreasonable Ones

chagriNed   gaSeous

(That's right; there seems to be no reason why the single letters are used, but there they are!)

•　　　　•　　　　•

Suggestion:

If you want to remember the exceptions, set up BONDS for them; then SEE and FEEL them:

1. The chanCELLor gave an exCELLent reason for his canCELLation of the talk on the plant CELL.

2. CrocheTed and ricocheTed suit me to a T.

3. He overlaPPed his authority and overstePPed his bounds.

4. I had to GRIN when he was chaGRINed.

5. GASeous is the adjective of GAS.

Suggestion:

Ordinarily, rules with many exceptions are worthless. That's why such rules have been left out of this book. Certainly, it's easier to use the SEE-THINK-FEEL method. However, the ACCENTED SYLLABLE rule works with so many hundreds of words that it's one you ought to make a real effort to learn. Give it a try.

FSA *equals* DOUBLE CONSONANT (before added syllable beginning with a vowel).

Now practice with these:

Word	Add: ED	Word	Add: ING
comMIT		beGIN	
conTROL		reFER	
Open		LEVel	
CAter		OFfer	

Word	Add: ER	Word	Add: ANCE
REVel		adMIT	
FAT		reMIT	

Word	Add: OR	Word	Add: ENCE
BET	_____	conFER	_____
			(Watch shift!)
EDit	_____	inFER	_____

Answers: committed, controlled, opened, catered, beginning, referring, leveling, offering, reveler, fatter, admittance, remittance, bettor, editor, conference, inference.

Now the review paragraphs. Don't try them until you have studied the material in this chapter carefully. One look is not enough. Only when you are sure of each section are you ready to test yourself. Remember: any mistakes, back you go to the explanation. The letter before each paragraph refers to the section where the words originally appeared in this chapter.

Review Paragraphs

A. Before going for his **laundry**, the **athlete** decided to attend the recent **film** which told the story of how **barbarous** tribes had once **attacked** the ancient Romans in the **disastrous** period of their decline. As he watched the picture, a **mischievous** little girl kept poking him with an **umbrella**. This proved quite a **hindrance** to his efforts to follow the scenes of **drowned** soldiers and burning houses. In his **remembrance**, he could not recall when he had been more annoyed.

_____

_____

_____

B. Dr. Jones **accidentally** dropped the box of **chocolates** on his way home from the **laboratory**. However, he still had the **jewelry** for his wife, along with the birthday **poem,** so he knew her **temperature** wouldn't rise.

C. Because of the **arctic** blasts common in **February,** it is no **surprise** that people recovering from **diphtheria** are told by doctors to stay indoors. In answer to a **question,** a **government** health agency agreed that this was wise. It would be almost **sacrilegious** to ignore both official and medical advice.

D. It is not **irrelevant** at this time to say that the **cavalry** has limited use today. The men who ride to war on horseback, however, do **perform** important jobs in hilly areas. Sending a tank up a steep pass would be inviting **tragedy.** With a little **perspiration** mounted troops overcome such obstacles.

_____

_____

_____

_____

_____

_____

E. School had begun to act like a sedative on Bob. Preparing sulphur in his chemistry class, struggling with arithmetic problems, or reading how the hypocrisy of certain kings had led to revolution no longer interested him. He prayed for an academic miracle which would make the compilation of facts a frivolous task and destroy the competition for marks which brought exultation only to the brighter students. There was consolation in the future, however. A relative had sent Bob an invitation to spend the summer on a ranch. He eagerly glanced over his uncle's narrative of what they would do out west. Now he could look forward to a definite celebration from school work.

F. The weather was almost perfect. Here and there slivers of sunlight shot through the stationary branches like silver darts. Everywhere I could hear birds calling to one another. There was also the croaking of frogs to add a bass section to the principal theme of the forest concert. I wondered whether I should waste my time scrawling words on the stationery that lay in my lap. Then I thought of George's last letter:

"It's clear that you're like most people without principle whose main job seems to be to excuse their failure to write. They're expert at telling what they should've done, but who's to say why they didn't. This is your last chance. No reply this time and you'd better forget my address and its owner!"

I put pen to paper. Nature would have to wait.

_____

_____

_____

G. The **editor opened** the **conference** by **leveling** a charge. Someone had **committed** the crime of **offering** a **bettor** a chance to make his profits **fatter** by showing him **preference** to **controlled** information. In fact, the **meeting** had been called by Mr. Grimes to mark the **beginning** of his campaign for **stopping** the release of news as it **occurred** and before it was **edited**.

"You can draw your own **inference**," he said. "I haven't **labeled** anyone, but it makes no **difference** to me who has **catered** to dishonest men. Whether he has received a **remittance** for his help or not, he will be **expelled**, and will never gain **admittance** to this office again. I'm **referring** to all when I say I would just as soon hire a drunken **reveler** as allow one of you to **flatten** the reputation of this paper. You've **batted** out of turn if you think I'm fooling."

Do not go on to the next chapter until you can spell each of the 89 key words correctly.

SEE THE WORD!

THINK THE WORD!

FEEL THE WORD!

SAY THE WORD!

and finally . . .

· VI ·

Build the Word!

A word is like a rubber band. It can be stretched, pushed together, or left in its original shape. Its job in a sentence determines what form it will take.

Love is not alone for the **lovely. Loveliness** of heart can **lovelier** be by far than of face, ofttimes **loved** briefly, but soon **loveless** and **lovelorn**—the **loveknot** broken, the **lovebird** flown, and the **lovers** parted. Then no **loving** hands will help the **lovesick** curl **lovable** hair into **lovelock** long.

This amorous adventure into word study brings us to the relationship between grammar and spelling. Writing a word correctly is sometimes only the beginning. It proves you know one form. However, you must learn all the other forms before you really have the situation and your spelling well in hand. You must become acquainted with a word's whole family tree, technically called the parts of speech. Let's see what the names of some of them are.

A. The Noun

This is the main thing we talk about in a sentence:

The **chair** is quite new.

or is part of a short group of words, called a phrase:

We walked (into the **woods**).

45

or may come at the end to help finish the thought:

I lifted the **box.**

or may appear in all three places at once:

The **launching** of the **ship** pleased the **town.**

Fundamentally, it is a name of:

1. A Person—**John** is my **brother.**
2. A Place—My **home** is in New York.
3. A Thing—A **shoe** is packed in a **box.**
4. An Idea—**Peace** feeds on **justice** and **understanding.**
5. An Activity—**Golf** is a good **sport.**

In brief, if it is a word which identifies anything you can see, hear, feel, taste, smell, or think about, it is a noun.

B. The Pronoun

Doesn't the following sound silly?

Mr. Mall rose from Mr. Mall's chair to get Mr. Mall's evening paper. Mr. Mall usually had it brought to Mr. Mall, but Mr. Mall had sent Mr. Mall's family on a visit to Mr. Mall's brother.

This sounds better:

Mr. Mall rose from his chair to get his evening paper. He usually had it brought to him, but he had sent his family on a visit to his brother.

The improvement was brought about by the use of pronouns. "Pro" comes from the Latin and means "instead of," or "for." Thus pronouns are used instead of nouns. There are three kinds of pronouns.

1. **Personal**—used instead of names readily identified.

   > I, me, we, us
   > you
   > he, him, she, her, it, they, them

   Example: See paragraph above.

2. **Indefinite**—as the term suggests, used when no one in particular is meant, but one person at a time is being considered.

   > each, either, neither, one
   > somebody, everybody, nobody, anybody
   > some one, everyone, no one, anyone

   Example: **Everybody** is eating his lunch.

3. **Relative**—used to refer to people or things **and** to connect one part of a sentence to another.

   > (for people) who, whoever, whosoever, whom, whomever, whomsoever
   > (for things) which
   > (for either) that

   Examples: Tom is the one **whom** I called. (or **that**)
   The suit **which** I want is expensive. (or **that**)

C. The Verb

The verb indicates what and when a noun or pronoun did something:

> The **lion** ROARED madly.

(Tells us what the lion—noun—did—at a previous date.)

or just makes a statement:

We ARE very tired.

(Enables us to make a statement about "We"—pronoun—at this moment.)

The verb may consist of *one word,* as above:

> or two: I have eaten already.
> or three: They have been traveling.
> or four: By this time Sunday, I shall have been fishing for two hours.

The verb sometimes changes when the number changes:

> Singular (one person, place, or thing, etc.): George walks to work.
> Plural (2 or more people, places, or things, etc.): They walk every day.

The verb also has tense, or indicates time:

> Tomorrow (future): shall or will paint, have painted, have been painting.
> Today (present): paints, paint, am, is, are painting.
> Yesterday (past): painted, was, were painting, has, have, had painted, has, have, had been painting.

D. The Adjective

If we had only the names for objects and people, our language would be dull, lack color and emotion. The adjective helps us get a better picture of a *noun or pronoun.* It may be directly attached to a word and influence its meaning:

I want a **large** piece of cake.
  (causes quantity to defeat manners)

She invited **only** me.
  (makes one exclusive)

or be separated from the word it influences by a verb:

That boy is **noisy**.
  (helps to warn one in advance)

The adjective may **merely describe**: tall man
or compare (**comparative degree**): taller than I
or select from 3 or more (**superlative degree**): **tallest** of the
group

E. The Adverb

Most frequently, the adverb gives us more information about a *verb*. That's why the "ad" syllable, meaning "toward, to," plus the "verb" is a very good definition in itself. Sometimes, however, the adverb may also describe an adjective or another adverb. Here are three examples:

1. Please tell the story **quickly**. ("tell" how?—information about a verb)
2. This table is **unusually** heavy. (how "heavy"?—information about an adjective)
3. She replied **rather** angrily. (how "angrily"?—information about an adverb)

The adverb may also **merely describe**: slowly
                          or compare: more slowly
                          or select from 3 or more: most slowly

·   ·   ·

There are other parts of speech, and books have been written on the principles of grammar that we have chosen *not* to discuss. But remember; we are interested in the subject only where it helps our spelling.

Certain helpful rules can be applied to words as they change from one part of speech to another. Study these rules carefully. Use them as further aids: Each shows how to BUILD THE WORD!

1. The "Y" Ending

When Y is preceded by a consonant, CHANGE Y TO I!

a. Nouns: When the plural is formed—

country, countries   pantry, pantries
city, cities   baby, babies

b. Verbs: When the tense changes—

try, tries, tried—BUT—trying (to avoid double I)
cry, cries, cried—BUT—crying (to avoid double I)
comply, complies, complied—BUT—complying (to avoid double I)
reply, replies, replied—BUT—replying (to avoid double I)

c. Adjectives:

hearty, heartier, heartiest
lazy, lazier, laziest
cozy, cozier, coziest
busy, busier, busiest (also noun: business)

d. Adverbs:

hearty, heartily   cozy, cozily
lazy, lazily   busy, busily

When Y is preceded by a vowel (a, e, i, o, u), KEEP the Y!

a. **Nouns: When the plural is formed—**

monkey, monkeys   donkey, donkeys
key, keys   alloy, alloys

b. **Verbs: When the tense changes—**

play, played, am playing, plays
survey, surveyed, was surveyed, surveys
lay, are laying, lays—BUT—laid, lain
slay, was slaying, slays—BUT—slain

c. **Adjectives and Adverbs:**

coy, coyly   boy, boyish, boyishly
cloy, cloying, cloyingly

d. **Two important exceptions:**

day, daily   gay, gaily

2. The Silent "E" Ending

Many words in the language end in E. Frequently, as in TAPE, SUPREME, KITE, ROPE, and USE, the letter is there to retain the "long" sound of the preceding vowel. At other times, there does not seem to be any good reason for its presence, as in SALVE, PROVE, SUITE, and LOVE, but it is there just the same. Because it only helps the sound of another letter, or is a useless remnant, it is called the SILENT VOWEL. When syllables are added to words ending in this silent E, special rules apply.

Example:

tribe	(silent E)
al	(syllable beginning with a vowel)
tribal	(THE SILENT E IS DROPPED WHEN A SYLLABLE BEGINNING WITH A VOWEL IS ADDED.)

Example:

grieve	
ance	
grievance	(THE SILENT E IS DROPPED.)

Try These:

Word	Add	
skate	ing	_____
blue	ish	_____
advise	ing	_____
	able	_____
use	able	_____
	age	_____
	ing	_____
console	ation	_____

Answers: skating, bluish, advising, advisable, usable, usage, using, consolation.

There are a few exceptions, but they are logical, so that you should remember them easily. If you have any trouble, fall back on the SEE-THINK-FEEL THE WORD treatment.

a. canoeing, hoeing—to avoid pronunciation difficulty, the E is retained. (also: shoe, toe)

b. dyeing, singeing—to avoid confusing them with **dying, singing,** the E is retained. (also: tinge)

c. CE and GE endings—to retain the sound of S in CE, and DJ in GE, the E is kept in the word. (serviceable, manageable, changeable, advantageous, courageous)

d. mileage—to avoid confusing it with **millage** (tax rate in mills per dollar) and to retain the long I sound, the E is kept.

The other part to this rule is not so reliable. When the silent E is followed by a syllable beginning with a consonant, the practice *generally* is to retain the E, as in GRATEFUL, LATELY, LAMENESS, ABATEMENT. There are numerous exceptions, however, and you are advised to check the individual words with a dictionary rather than depend on the rule. Watch out particularly for ARGUMENT, JUDGMENT, and ACKNOWLEDGMENT. And make sure you spell SINCERELY and NINETEEN correctly; they *do* follow the rule. Lastly, DEVELOPMENT has nothing to do with the rule at all since the original word is DEVELOP (no silent E ending)!

3. The "LY" Ending

The most frequent use of the LY syllable is to change adjectives into adverbs. When you are in doubt about the spelling of a word ending in LY:

a. Write the adjective form first.

b. Check the last letter.

If it is Y, treat it like any Y ending.

| necessary | Y to I | necessarily |
| heavy | Y to I | heavily |

If it is LE, change E to Y and that's all!

| considerable | E to Y | considerably |
| capable | E to Y | capably |

If it is L, leave it there!

| usual | L stays | usually |
| oral | L stays | orally |

If it is E, leave it there!

| extreme | E stays | extremely |
| late | E stays | lately |

Add LY to these:

satisfactory	_____	definite	_____
merry	_____	absolute	_____
happy	_____	sincere	_____
personal	_____	able	_____
natural	_____	double	_____
awful	_____	subtle	_____

Answers: satisfactorily, merrily, happily, personally, naturally, awfully, definitely, absolutely, sincerely, ably, doubly, subtly.

4. The "ABLE-IBLE" Endings

This rule isn't foolproof. However, it will work 99% of the time. The occasional exception? Give it the treatment!

a. If you can form a word ending in IVE or SION, use IBLE.

permission	permissible
divisive	divisible
resistive	resistible, irresistible
reversion	reversible
conversion	convertible

b. If you cannot, use ABLE.

depend	dependable
use	usable (silent E dropped)
sale	salable
receive	receivable
commend	commendable

c. Here are two exceptions you can give the treatment at once:

feasible	remittable

5. The "C" Ending

Notice these two examples:

colic, colicky   picnic, picnicked, picnicking

The K is added before the final syllable to prevent the C's being sounded like an S.

Try it with these:

shellac, panic, traffic
(Add ING, ED, ER, or Y, if possible)

Answers: shellacking, shellacked, panicked, panicky, trafficking, trafficked.

6. The "FULL" Ending

In general, when you add this syllable to a word, omit one of the L's.

hope, hopeful   skill, skillful, skilful
spite, spiteful   fate, fateful

7. The "SEDE, CEED, CEDE" Endings

a. Only one word in the language uses S:
   superSede

b. Three words use CEED:
   proCEED, sucCEED, exCEED

c. All others use CEDE:
   reCEDE   preCEDE
   conCEDE   interCEDE, etc.

8. Unusual Plural Endings

a. "O"

If the singular form ends in an O preceded by a consonant, usually add ES.

echo, echoes   potato, potatoes
Negro, Negroes   cargo, cargoes

If the singular form ends in an O preceded by a vowel, always add only S.

cameo, cameos   patio, patios
studio, studios   ratio, ratios

Also:

musical terms—altos, sopranos
clipped words—photos, autos
recent words—gauchos, commandos

b. "Y"

We have already covered this:

Y preceded by a consonant, change Y to I, and add ES.
Y preceded by a vowel, add only S.

puppy, puppies   relay, relays
berry, berries   convoy, convoys

c. Irregular Nouns

Words taken from a foreign language often present problems. No general rules exist, so that each one must be
checked with a dictionary. The best approach here, too, is the
SEE-THINK-FEEL treatment.

hippopotamus, hippopotamuses, hippopotami
alumnus, alumni (male), alumna, alumnae (female)
phenomenon, phenomena

9. Front Syllables

So far we have been talking about spelling problems
that are created by the addition of syllables at the ends
of words. Many errors occur also at the beginnings,
especially when the question of doubling a letter arises.
You can handle these without trouble if you use this
method:

a. Single Letter

disappear

A common misspelling of this word is to use an extra S.
Here's what to do:

Separate the first syllable from the basic word:

dis appear

What does it end with? S.
What does the rest begin with? A.
Any double letter? NO!

Again:

    dis appoint   disappoint

Ends-S   Begins-A   Double? NO!

  b. Double Letter

    misspell

Separate the first syllable from the basic word:

    mis spell

What does it end with? S.
What does the rest begin with? S.
Any double letter? YES! Double S.

Again:

    dis service   disservice

Ends-S   Begins-S   Double? YES!

A few more of both kinds:

un necessary	unnecessary
re commend	recommend
dis approve	disapprove
a cross	across
ad dress	address

10. Hyphenated Expressions

The tendency today is to use the hyphen (-) as little as possible. In fact, experts who prefer its use have been unable to agree on a set of rules. Therefore, when you aren't sure, leave out the hyphen. These are the preferred uses on which there is general agreement.

a. Fused Adjectives, Numbers

   i. Several words combined to form one adjective:
      never-to-be-forgotten day
      well-executed double play

   ii. Twenty-one, thirty-three, etc., up to ninety-nine

b. "Ex" and "Self"

When these syllables are attached to the beginning of a word, use the hyphen.

   ex-private   self-appointed   ex-counterman

c. Before a capital letter or a similar vowel

   un-American   re-echo
   pro-British   co-owner

11. The Apostrophe (')

This symbol is used in a variety of situations. If you omit a necessary apostrophe, you have misspelled the word, even though the error did not involve a letter.

a. To Indicate Possession, Ownership

This is its major use. Here, too, there is a lack of agreement among the experts. Fortunately, the easiest rule to apply also happens to be the most modern. Use this method and, if someone shows you another way, tell him you prefer to be up-to-date.

   i. If the word ends in S, use only (').

      Boys play games. I enjoy watching boys' games.
      Charles had a hat. Who took Charles' hat?
      Have you read Dickens' "A Tale of Two Cities"?

ii. If the word does **not end in S**, use ('S).

> These are children's toys.
> We looked for the girl's blue coat.
> Ladies will exercise a lady's privilege.

iii. In groups of two or more, last member receives mark.

> It's occupied by Chisholm and Boone's law firm.
> I'm tired of every Tom, Dick, and Harry's complaint.

iv. In hyphenated expressions, place mark at end.

> She visited her son-in-law's house.
> Ask the sergeant-at-arms' permission.

v. Use mark on noun or pronoun attached to words ending in "ing." (No mark for personal pronouns)

> They discussed **Cole's** leaving the force.
> I wondered whether **someone else's** winning would upset her.
> They didn't approve of **my** going.

Important! Remember these personal pronouns **never use the apostrophe!**

mine, ours	yours
his, hers, its	theirs
whose	

b. Plurals of Letters, Numbers, and Words Used As Words

> How many "r's" does the word have?
> There are three 2's in my number.
> The company's president used too many "and's" in his speech.

c. Contractions:
See Chapter V, p. 33.

12. Capital Letters

Good spelling habits require that you use these carefully.

a. Titles of Books, Plays, Articles, Newspapers, Magazines, etc.

The first and last words of a title are always written with capital letters. In the rest, only articles (a, an, the), prepositions (of, by, to), and conjunctions (and, if, as), when they are shorter than four letters, may be written without capitals.

> The Taming of the Shrew
> The Shape of Things to Come
> What Men Live By

b. Proper Nouns

Any word that becomes the name of a particular place, person, or thing should be capitalized. Very often, the same word may be either proper or common.

Observe:

> He bought a piece of **territory** in the **northwest** part of the state.
> The establishment of the **Northwest Territory** raised controversial issues.
> People who live in the **north** frequently go to the **south** in the winter.
> The Civil War involved the **North** against the **South**.

Note:

When a proper noun becomes an adjective, the capital letter is retained.

> France is the place to study **French** customs.

If you plan to travel to South America, learn the **Span-ish** language.

It was a wallop of **Ruthian** proportions.

c. First Words

Lines of Poetry

"Take her up tenderly,
 Lift her with care,
 Fashioned so slenderly,
 Young and so fair."

Direct Quotations

"Off with her head!" shouted Henry.
Henry shouted, "Off with her head!"

Salutations, Closings of Letters

Dear Mr. Smith:
Sincerely yours,

Rewrite the following, inserting all capital letters that have been left out:

> 72 ellen drive
> rockaway, new jersey
> january 6, 1954

dear john,

when i spoke to you about "south pacific" i didn't realize that your french cousin had expressed a de-sire to go, too. well, as shakespeare said,

"let me not to the marriage of true minds
 admit impediments"

in this case i'll be preacher jones, and perform the ceremony of wedding broadway to gallic charm.

> cordially,
> horton

Now check:

> 72 Ellen Drive
> Rockaway, New Jersey
> January 6, 1954

Dear John,

When I spoke to you about "South Pacific" I didn't realize that your French cousin had expressed a desire to go, too. Well, as Shakespeare said,

"Let me not to the marriage of true minds
Admit impediments"

In this case I'll be Preacher Jones and perform the ceremony of wedding Broadway to Gallic charm.

> Cordially,
> Horton

The review paragraphs in this chapter will contain samplings, rather than the complete list of words used as illustration. You understand, of course, that the main stress was on rules rather than on individual words. Your knowledge of these (and some exceptions) is what we want to test.

Special Endings

Willie almost **cried** when he came face to face with the **monkeys.** For some reason, they reminded him of furry **babies,** but the way they **lazily surveyed** him made him feel sure they were very old. Suddenly, Uncle Jasper invited Willie to go **canoeing.** It was a **commendable** suggestion meant to keep the boy **manageable.** However, it was going to be **extremely** difficult to start the trip **happily** because at the moment tears seemed **irresistible.** Suddenly again, two astounding **phenomena interceded** in **panicky** Willie's behalf. First, a group of **sopranos**, sitting in a **convertible**, drove by, singing "Lonesome **Cargoes**." Then, a **tribal** chieftain, wearing a string of **cameos**, **skillfully** began leading two **hippopota- muses** into a dance. So **advantageous** was this welcome change that Willie allowed a **grateful** grin to **supersede** his **boyishly** sad expression. Then Willie woke up. It had been a dreadful nightmare.

Front Syllables, Hyphens, Apostrophes

What is meant by the term **"un-American"**? Well, **it's** many things. One who **disapproves** of **everyone's** right to speak freely is offering a **disservice** to his country. The **self-ap- pointed** critic of **another's** beliefs acts **unpatriotically** when he **recommends** that even a **person's** thinking should be con- trolled. Abraham Lincoln, in several **addresses**, spoke of the need for **well-developed** citizens from **twenty-one** to **seventy- one** who would become **co-owners** of a country that accepted every **Tom, Dick,** and **Harry's** differences, allowed no **"anti's"** to develop against any group, and used the three **"r's"** to be watchful of your interests and **theirs**. In this way, fearing some **so-called** strong man would become **unnecessary**. **Unable** to make headway, such an individual would quickly learn that a **dictator's** hand could not reach **across** the land without **its** being broken.

In the foregoing paragraphs there are fifty key words. If you miss any, go back and study the rules which apply to your error.

_____

_____

_____

_____

_____

_____

_____

_____

The last two chapters have thrown rules at you by the handful. Perhaps by now you wish you had skipped them. There are so many things to remember.

It isn't really that bad. Bear in mind that the majority of words cannot be classified. They require individual study. You know how to do that. If you prefer to use the SEE-THINK-FEEL method for all words, fine! Any rule that *bothers you* isn't worth *bothering with*. If you can remember the rule easily, and it helps, use it. If you can't, forget the rule and treat each word by itself.

· VII ·

The Treatment

Six Minutes A Day!

It's time to take stock. You now know the basic system which can be *applied to any word:*

SEE THE WORD!

Get a picture in your mind, especially of the difficult part of the word.

THINK THE WORD!

Prepare some bit of easily-remembered nonsense for the troublesome syllable or letter.

FEEL THE WORD!

Trace the word WITH YOUR FINGER, and learn to write it while concentrating on something else.

You are also familiar with the devices for handling large groups of words:

SAY THE WORD!

Be careful not to leave out, add, or confuse syllables and letters. Use other words in the same family to locate key vowels in words. Be careful of words that sound alike. Learn the ACCENTED SYLLABLE RULE! FSA!

BUILD THE WORD!

Follow the changes in spelling from one part of speech to another. Study unusual plurals, front and back syllables, hyphens, possessives, and capital letters.

These are the five simple steps we mentioned in the first chapter. Together they are the tested way to make the correct spelling of any word a lifelong habit. Now we are going to prescribe a simple six minute a day program to make sure that good spelling stays with you forever.

DAILY PROGRAM

Time	Procedure
MORNING	A. Look up the pronunciation of your troublesome word in a good dictionary.
3 Minutes	SAY THE WORD. Then observe how it is built. Set up the image to SEE THE WORD. Stare at it for ten seconds. Look away at another surface. Count five; "see" the image with your mind. Write the word rapidly. (90 seconds)
	B. Prepare the BOND. THINK THE WORD. Write the word as you think of the association. (30 seconds)

C. Write the word in large script letters.

FEEL THE WORD by tracing it three times with your finger.

Say each letter aloud as you trace.

Write the word rapidly, and, as you do, say anything that comes into your mind, or repeat the association. (60 seconds)

AFTERNOON   Repeat the entire procedure outlined above, except for looking the word up in the dictionary.

1 Minute,   This should take about half the time it took
   30 seconds   you in the morning since you are simply recalling what you have done.

Do not skip any steps. It will require patience, but stay with it.

EVENING   Repeat everything once more.

1 Minute,   Don't try more than ONE WORD A DAY.
   30 seconds   Anything more will divide your attention, and reduce the single effect you want to establish.

With this plan you can cover five words from Monday to Friday. Use the week end for review by preparing a few sentences or a paragraph which contains the words you studied that week. Ask someone to dictate the material, if possible.

In the next chapter you will find a ninety day trial which uses the six minute a day routine so, before you go ahead, make certain you understand this simple program.

· VIII ·

Ninety Day Trial

No one gets to be a good golfer simply by listening to a professional, nor, for that matter, simply by reading a book. By itself the best instruction in the world does not substantially improve a student's skill. The difference between the person who "knows how" and the person who "can do" is quite obviously practice, practice, and more practice. This is as true of spelling as it is of golf, or tennis, or bridge, or learning to play the piano.

Strangely enough, moreover, spelling is one of the few fields where practice really *does* make perfect . . . and where perfection is the only thing that counts. For example, if you sink nine putts out of ten in golf you are considered an extraordinarily good golfer. But in spelling you don't win any prizes for getting nine letters right in a ten letter word. You either spell a word perfectly or you misspell it. There is no comparative degree in the game of spelling.

What follows therefore is a practice session. It is also a ninety day trial by which you can prove to yourself that good spellers are made, not born.

Ninety days may sound like a long stretch, but actually the total time you'll have to devote to practice equals only nine hours or slightly more than one working day. It is little enough to ask when you consider the goal: to make you a perfect speller.

The practice list for the ninety day trial consists of sixty words. These so-called demons are not particularly unusual or difficult, but they are commonly misspelled by more than 25% of educated people.

You may already know how to spell some of the words. If you do, cross out the ones that have been offered and write in the substitutes you have chosen from the lists provided in the appendix. The individual words are important, but the most important thing is the steady, planned attack. Because once you've become experienced, *any* spelling demon can be tamed by giving it the treatment.

Take one word a day and spend six minutes on it. Study each exactly as described in "THE TREATMENT." Cover five words a week. Use Saturdays and Sundays for review. At the end of each month, do the test on the month's twenty words. If you miss any, don't go ahead until your score is 100%.

Here are seven important suggestions which will help you start on the right road:

1. Before you proceed with a word, check its pronunciation in a dictionary, **even if you think you know it;** then write it in pencil in the space provided on each page that follows. I have deliberately omitted this information so that you will train yourself to use the dictionary often as the final authority on the spoken word.

2. Use the spaces under "Image" for additional diagrams you may think of, under "Bond" for further nonsense associations, and under "Trace" for writing the word in script during the daily review. **Your own handwriting** should form the basis for the tracing practice.

3. Use the fifteen sentences for the week-end reviews. Take ten (two for each word) on Saturday, and five (one for each word) on Sunday. Have someone dictate them, or glance rapidly at each, memorize it, and then write it.

4. A notation like "VI—Front Syllables" refers to the rule or suggestion covered in the chapter indicated by the Roman numeral. Review the section as you practice.

5. If possible, form a team with another person working on spelling. Help each other by exchanging dictation of test paragraphs and sentences. Write weekly letters in which you purposely use newly-learned words.

6. Do not assume that you need peace and quiet for your practice sessions. Train yourself to concentrate even in the midst of great noise and confusion. Make your spelling automatic!

7. Before you start be sure you understand and can apply the techniques discussed in previous chapters. Also be certain you can follow the six minute a day program. Once you do start, don't let yourself give up. Be serious. Be faithful. Six minutes each day. That's all.

FIRST WEEK: Monday
Word 1:   co op er a tion

Pronunciation: _____

Image: COOPeration
  See A,
  page 67   _____

               _____

               _____

Bond: I need your COOPeration to clean the
  See B,   COOP.
  page 67   See VI—Front Syllables

               _____

               _____

               _____

Trace: _cooperation_
  See C,
  page 68   _____

               _____

               _____

Sentences: **Cooperation** among nations will lead to
               peace.
                    I offer my **cooperation** gladly.
                    A good team depends upon **cooperation**.

FIRST WEEK: Tuesday
Word 2: ac quaint ance

Pronunciation: _____

Image: acQUAINTAnce

_____

_____

_____

Bond: He speaks with a QUAINT A.

_____

_____

_____

Trace: *acquaintance*

_____

_____

_____

Sentences: My **acquaintance** is coming to see me.
Give me an **acquaintance**, and I'll make
him a friend.
A smile and a greeting can make an
acquaintance.

FIRST WEEK: Wednesday
Word 3:   gov ern ment

Pronunciation: _____

Image: goVERNment

                 _____

                 _____

                 _____

Bond: VERN Porter works for the goVERN-
                 ment.
                 See V—Omitted Syllables

                 _____

                 _____

                 _____

Trace: *government*

                 _____

                 _____

                 _____

Sentences: **Government** separates men from beasts.
                 Only a weak **government** permits in-
                 flation.
                 Your ballot helps you control your **gov-
                 ernment.**

FIRST WEEK:	Thursday
Word 4:	re quire ment

Pronunciation: _____

Image: reQUIREment

_____

_____

_____

Bond: A QUIRE of paper will meet my re-QUIREment.
See VI—Silent "E" Ending

_____

_____

_____

Trace: *requirement*

_____

_____

_____

Sentences: One **requirement** is a local address.
If you meet the **requirement**, you will be accepted.
No one is permitted to ignore a **requirement**.

FIRST WEEK: Friday
Word 5:   ex cel lent

Pronunciation: _____

Image: exCELLEnt

              _____

              _____

              _____

Bond: The prisoner in CELL E shows ex-
              CELLEnt conduct.

              _____

              _____

              _____

Trace: _excellent_

              _____

              _____

              _____

Sentences: **Excellent** apples can be bought now.
              She has an **excellent** program arranged
              for us.
              The fishing in this lake is **excellent**.

Review: 10 Sentences on Saturday

_____

_____

_____

_____

_____

_____

_____

_____

_____

5 Sentences on Sunday

_____

_____

_____

_____

_____

SECOND WEEK: Monday
Word 6:   def i nite

Pronunciation: _____

Image: defInIte

                _____

                _____

                _____

Bond: An I for an I is a defInIte Biblical
                saying.

                _____

                _____

Trace: *definite*

                _____

                _____

                _____

Sentences: **Definite** signs of spring are here.
                Give me a **definite** answer, please.
                He could not make the time **definite**.

SECOND WEEK: Tuesday
Word 7:   cat a log

Pronunciation: _____

Image: catALOG

                  _____

                  _____

                  _____

Bond: You will find even A LOG for sale in
                  the catALOG.

                  _____

                  _____

                  _____

Trace: *catalog*

                  _____

                  _____

                  _____

Sentences: Catalog these prices for the next issue.
                  You will find this catalog in many Amer-
                  ican homes.
                  Let's take a look in the catalog.

SECOND WEEK: Wednesday

Word 8:   sense

Pronunciation: _____

Image: seNSe

                        _____

                        _____

                        _____

Bond: NS means "no seNSe."

                        _____

                        _____

                        _____

Trace: _____ *sense* _____

                        _____

                        _____

                        _____

Sentences: Sense comes with experience.
                        He could sense the coming storm.
                        Avoid accidents by using common sense.

SECOND WEEK: Thursday
Word 9:   bul le tin

Pronunciation: _____

Image: BULLETIN
                     _____
                     _____
                     _____

Bond: The BULLET lodged IN the BULLE-
                     TIN board.
                     _____
                     _____
                     _____

Trace: *bulletin*
                     _____
                     _____
                     _____

Sentences: Bulletin 9 will be issued on Monday.
                     This is a bulletin from the front.
                     Tack this on the bulletin board.

SECOND WEEK: Friday
Word 10:   oc ca sion

Pronunciation: _____

Image: oCCasion

                  _____

                  _____

                  _____

Bond: A 2 CC dose will do for this oCCasion.

                  _____

                  _____

                  _____

Trace: *occasion*

                  _____

                  _____

                  _____

Sentences: An **occasion** like this will be long re-
                  membered.
                  Let me take this **occasion** to thank you.
                  I'm sure it will be a great **occasion**.

Review: 10 Sentences on Saturday

_____

_____

_____

_____

_____

_____

_____

_____

_____

_____

5 Sentences on Sunday

_____

_____

_____

_____

_____

THIRD WEEK: Monday

Word 11: rec om men da tion

Pronunciation: _____

Image: reCoMMendation

_____

_____

_____

Bond: I C the MM's in reCoMMendation.
See VI—Front Syllables

_____

_____

_____

Trace: *recommendation*

_____

_____

_____

Sentences: **Recommendation** is essential for a job.
I shall give my **recommendation** when
it is asked.
Send in your **recommendation**.

THIRD WEEK: Tuesday
Word 12: fi nan cial

Pronunciation: _____

Image: fINANcial

_____

_____

_____

Bond: FINANcial success begins IN AN account with a bank.

_____

_____

_____

Trace: _____ *financial* _____

_____

_____

_____

Sentences: **Financial** news is found in most newspapers.

What is the **financial** rating of this company?

The nature of this report is **financial.**

THIRD WEEK: Wednesday
Word 13: de ter mine

Pronunciation: _____

Image: deterMINE

_____

_____

_____

Bond: MINE will deterMINE the final result.

_____

_____

_____

Trace: *determine*

_____

_____

_____

Sentences: **Determine** the answer by dividing.
When did he **determine** to follow this policy?
I wish I knew what the fates will **determine.**

THIRD WEEK: Thursday
Word 14:   nec es sar y

Pronunciation: _____

Image: neCESSary

               _____

               _____

               _____

Bond: It is neCESSary to keep a CESS pool
               clean.

               _____

               _____

               _____

Trace: _____ *necessary* _____

               _____

               _____

               _____

Sentences: **Necessary** steps are being taken.
               It won't be **necessary** for you to come.
               I wonder whether that was **necessary**.

THIRD WEEK: Friday
Word 15:   quan ti ty

Pronunciation: _____

Image: quANTITY

_____

_____

_____

Bond: A quANTITY of ants might be called an ANTITY.

_____

_____

_____

Trace: *quantity*

_____

_____

_____

Sentences: **Quantity** is what we need now.
The same **quantity** sold for less.
I want a greater **quantity**.

Review: 10 Sentences on Saturday

_____

_____

_____

_____

_____

_____

_____

_____

_____

_____

5 Sentences on Sunday

_____

_____

_____

_____

_____

FOURTH WEEK: Monday
Word 16:   con science

Pronunciation: _____

Image: conSCIENCE

_____

_____

_____

Bond: CON plus SCIENCE equals CON-
SCIENCE.

_____

_____

_____

Trace: *conscience*

_____

_____

_____

Sentences: "**Conscience** makes cowards of us all."
Let your **conscience** be your guide.
He knew this would not satisfy his
conscience.

FOURTH WEEK: Tuesday
Word 17: au thor i ty

Pronunciation: _____

Image: auTHORity

_____

_____

_____

Bond: The god THOR was an ancient symbol of auTHORity.

_____

_____

_____

Trace: *authority*

_____

_____

_____

Sentences: **Authority** should rest with the wise and just.
You have no **authority** to do that.
You will have to state your **authority**.

FOURTH WEEK: Wednesday
Word 18: ben e fit

Pronunciation: _____

Image: benEFit

_____

_____

_____

Bond: Sound and spell the EF in benEFit.

_____

_____

_____

Trace: *benefit*

_____

_____

_____

Sentences: **Benefit** yourself by checking the value.
Of what **benefit** will this be?
His major interest was the public **bene-fit**.

FOURTH WEEK: Thursday
Word 19:   ba sis

Pronunciation: _____

Image: baSIS

                    _____
                    _____
                    _____

Bond: Billy was punished on the baSIS of what
                    SIS said.

                    _____
                    _____
                    _____

Trace: _basis_____

                    _____
                    _____
                    _____

Sentences: The **basis** for his action was the report.
                    You have no **basis** for your complaint.
                    The loan will require a sound **basis**.

FOURTH WEEK: Friday
Word 20:   ex ist ence

Pronunciation: _____

Image: exisTENce

                _____

                _____

                _____

Bond: This firm has been in exisTENce for
                TEN years.

                _____

                _____

                _____

Trace: *existence*

                _____

                _____

                _____

Sentences: Existence is the first desire of mankind.
                I did not know of the existence of this
                product.
                How long has it been in existence?

Review: 15 Sentences on Saturday

_____

_____

_____

_____

_____

_____

_____

1 Paragraph (next page)
Sunday Morning

_____

_____

_____

1 Paragraph Sunday Evening

_____

_____

_____

_____

Review Paragraphs: First Month

Each paragraph covers words 1-20. If you miss any in the first, study them carefully, one a day in the regular way; then try the second paragraph.

I.

If we were to **catalog** the **requirements** of good **government,** we would list certain **definite** points. There would have to be one person in **authority** whose good **sense** would inspire **cooperation** on every **occasion.** He would handle a **bulletin** from abroad with the same clear **conscience** as he would a **financial** problem at home. No mere **acquaintance** would be able to **benefit** on the **basis** of friendship, nor would a party **recommendation** be **necessary** to **determine** fitness for office. Unfortunately there is no great **quantity** of such **excellent** men in **existence.**

II.

The **existence** of the mail order **catalog** has been of **benefit** to many people for years. **Government** workers, whose **financial** position is never among the highest, can buy **necessary** items at fair prices because the **basis** on which these companies operate is **quantity** sales, **excellent** materials, and low profit **requirements.** To **determine** the **definite** aid this type of selling is to others as well, one may read the **recommendations** that appear in **bulletins** issued by consumer organizations whose **authority** and **cooperation** are sought by persons of good **sense** all over the country. On one **occasion,** an **acquaintance** of mine remarked that the public **conscience** made business through the mails possible.

FIFTH WEEK: Monday
Word 21: per ma nent

Pronunciation: _____

Image: perMANEnt

_____
_____
_____

Bond: The MANE is a perMANEnt part of a lion.

_____
_____
_____

Trace: *permanent*

_____
_____
_____

Sentences: **Permanent** plans were made.

This is a **permanent** part of the building.

This time we'll make it **permanent**.

FIFTH WEEK: Tuesday
Word 22: ac com mo date

Pronunciation: _____

Image: aCCoMModate

_____

_____

_____

Bond: "The Double C-Modern Motel" We aCCoMModate 50 guests.

_____

_____

_____

Trace: *accommodate*

_____

_____

_____

Sentences: **Accommodate** me by changing this bill, please.

We cannot **accommodate** you before Monday.

How many do you think they will **accommodate**?

FIFTH WEEK: Wednesday
Word 23:   ex ten sion

Pronunciation: _____

Image: exTENSion

_____

_____

_____

Bond: The exTENSion will cost TENS of thousands.

_____

_____

_____

Trace: *extension*

_____

_____

_____

Sentences: **Extension** of your credit is not possible.
I shall need the **extension** for an extra bedroom.
What is the number of the **extension**?

FIFTH WEEK: Thursday
Word 24:   mis chief

Pronunciation: _____

Image: misCHIEF

                    _____

                    _____

                    _____

Bond: He was the CHIEF cause of the mis-
                    CHIEF.

                    _____

                    _____

                    _____

Trace: _____ *mischief* _____

                    _____

                    _____

                    _____

Sentences: **Mischief** is common to small boys.
                    It was the kind of **mischief** that had to
                    be stopped.
                    Now don't you get into any **mischief**.

FIFTH WEEK: Friday
Word 25: A mer i can

Pronunciation: _____

Image: AmERICan

_____

_____

_____

Bond: ERIC is now an AmERICan.

_____

_____

_____

Trace: *American*

_____

_____

_____

Sentences: **American** ideals are founded on free-dom.

He is an **American** by birth.

To be selfish is to be un-**American**.

Review: 10 Sentences on Saturday

_____

_____

_____

_____

_____

_____

_____

_____

5 Sentences on Sunday

_____

_____

_____

_____

_____

SIXTH WEEK: Monday
Word 26:   ex ec u tive

Pronunciation: _____

Image: exeCUTive

              _____

              _____

              _____

Bond: The exeCUTive got a CUT on his arm.

              _____

              _____

              _____

Trace: *executive*

              _____

              _____

              _____

Sentences: **Executive** talent is a rare thing.
              He is an **executive** for a large company.
              That's the name of the new **executive**.

SIXTH WEEK: Tuesday

Word 27: thor ough

Pronunciation: _____

Image: thoROUGH

_____

_____

_____

Bond: It was a ROUGH but thoROUGH job.

_____

_____

_____

Trace: *thorough*

_____

_____

_____

Sentences: **Thorough** work is necessary in science.

It was a **thorough** success from the beginning.

That report seems to be very **thorough**.

SIXTH WEEK: Wednesday
Word 28: par tial

Pronunciation: _____

Image: PARTial

_____

_____

_____

Bond: A PART is a PARTial amount.

_____

_____

_____

Trace: *partial*

_____

_____

_____

Sentences: Partial payment is not enough.
Try not to be **partial** in your attitude.
The score shows that you have a **partial.**

SIXTH WEEK: Thursday
Word 29: bas ket ball

Pronunciation: _____

Image: BASKETball

_____

_____

_____

Bond: A BASKET and a BALL are the tools of BASKETball.

_____

_____

_____

Trace: *basketball*

_____

_____

_____

Sentences: Basketball is an American game.
He plays basketball in the winter.
I went to see a game of basketball.

SIXTH WEEK: Friday
Word 30: judg ment

Pronunciation: _____

Image: judGMent

_____

_____

_____

Bond: Good judGMent is found in **Good Men.**

_____

_____

_____

Trace: *judgment*

_____

_____

_____

Sentences: **Judgment** was pronounced the follow-
ing day.
He used his **judgment** in deciding.
This will need careful **judgment.**

Review: 10 Sentences on Saturday

_____

_____

_____

_____

_____

_____

_____

_____

_____

5 Sentences on Sunday

_____

_____

_____

_____

_____

SEVENTH WEEK: Monday
Word 31:   ca pac i ty

Pronunciation: _____

Image: capaCITY

_____

_____

_____

Bond: The CITY was filled to capaCITY.

_____

_____

_____

Trace: *capacity*

_____

_____

_____

Sentences: **Capacity** business was being done.
                What is the **capacity** of the room?
                We ought to know the **capacity**.

SEVENTH WEEK: Tuesday

Word 32:   war rant

Pronunciation: _____

Image: WARRANt

_____

_____

_____

Bond: During the WAR he RAN from a WAR-
RANt officer.

_____

_____

_____

Trace: *warrant*

_____

_____

_____

Sentences: A **warrant** for his arrest was issued.
Do you **warrant** the contents of this
product?
I cannot honor this **warrant**.

SEVENTH WEEK: Wednesday

Word 33:   lit er a ture

Pronunciation: _____

Image: litERAture

                  _____

                  _____

                  _____

Bond: This ERA has produced good litERA-
                  ture.

                  _____

                  _____

                  _____

Trace: *literature*

                  _____

                  _____

                  _____

Sentences: **Literature** delights the mind.
                  The study of **literature** is required in
                  college.
                  Every war produces its own **literature**.

SEVENTH WEEK: Thursday
Word 34:   crit i cism

Pronunciation: _____

Image: CRITICism

                  _____

                  _____

                  _____

Bond: A CRITIC offers CRITICism.

                  _____

                  _____

                  _____

Trace: *criticism*

                  _____

                  _____

                  _____

Sentences: **Criticism** can promote growth.

                  Do not accept **criticism** from the unin-
                  formed.

                  He conducts a column of dramatic
                  criticism.

SEVENTH WEEK: Friday
Word 35:   in ter rupt

Pronunciation: _____

Image: intERRupt

_____
_____
_____

Bond: You ERR when you intERRupt.

_____
_____

Trace: _interrupt_

_____
_____
_____

Sentences: **Interrupt** me when the time is up.
If you **interrupt** him he will become angry.
I don't think they should **interrupt**.

Review: 10 Sentences on Saturday

_____

_____

_____

_____

_____

_____

_____

_____

_____

_____

5 Sentences on Sunday

_____

_____

_____

_____

_____

EIGHTH WEEK: Monday
Word 36:   zo ol o gy

Pronunciation: _____

Image: ZOOlogy

                _____
                _____
                _____

Bond: Study ZOOlogy in a ZOO.
                See VI—Front Syllables

                _____
                _____
                _____

Trace: _*zoology*_____
                _____
                _____
                _____

Sentences: **Zoology** is the science of animal life.
                A course in **zoology** will be given this
                fall.
                "Zoo" comes from the first syllable of
                zoology.

EIGHTH WEEK: Tuesday

Word 37:   as cer tain

Pronunciation: _____

Image: asCERTAIN

                      _____

                      _____

                      _____

Bond: When you ASCERTAIN you become
                      AS CERTAIN as possible.

                      _____

                      _____

                      _____

Trace: _____ *ascertain* _____

                      _____

                      _____

                      _____

Sentences: **Ascertain** the truth of the statement.
                      I cannot **ascertain** the real reason.
                      This is something I must **ascertain**.

EIGHTH WEEK: Wednesday
Word 38: trea son

Pronunciation: _____

Image: tREASON

_____

_____

_____

Bond: There is no good REASON for tREA-SON.

_____

_____

_____

Trace: _treason_

_____

_____

_____

Sentences: Treason can be punished by death.
"If this be treason, make the most of it."
Selling official information is an act of treason.

EIGHTH WEEK: Thursday
Word 39:   ex haust ed

Pronunciation: _____

Image: exHAUSted

          _____
          _____
          _____

Bond: **HA,** you have not ex **HAUS**ted **US.**

          _____
          _____
          _____

Trace: *exhausted*

          _____
          _____
          _____

Sentences: **Exhausted,** he just sat there.
              You have **exhausted** me, my boy.
              That comedian leaves me **exhausted.**

EIGHTH WEEK: Friday
Word 40: dor mi to ry

Pronunciation: _____

Image: dORMITOry

_____
_____
_____

Bond: Mrs. ORMITO ran the dORMITOry.

_____
_____
_____

Trace: _*dormitory*_

_____
_____
_____

Sentences: **Dormitory** rules were very strict.
This is the **dormitory** for men.
The party took place in the **dormitory**.

Review: 15 Sentences on Saturday

_____

_____

_____

_____

_____

_____

_____

1 Paragraph (next page)
Sunday Morning

_____

_____

_____

1 Paragraph Sunday Evening

_____

_____

_____

_____

Review Paragraphs: Second Month

The first paragraph covers words 21-40. The second offers you another look at 1-20. Should you miss any, be sure to go over them again (as if they were new words) before you continue with the next set.

I.

It took a **basketball** scandal to awaken the **American** public to the fact that **mischief** can be spread in any **dormitory**. It is easy to hurl **criticism** at officials who lacked good **judgment**, or even at the high **executive** who was blind to the **treason** being committed under his very nose. However, the **permanent** cure is not to be found in an **extension** of the investigation but in a **thorough** return to the real purpose of education. The **exhausted** rooter should be taught that his **capacity** for wise living and his ability to **ascertain** how he can fit the needs of society will best be developed by the study of subjects like **literature**, history, **mathematics**, and **zoology** than by the size of the score of his favorite team. Sports should not **interrupt** the basic program, but should become a **partial** relief from the daily grind. Let the desire to **accommodate** the athletic hero not lead to a **warrant** for his arrest on charges of bribery.

II.

A **bulletin** from the **financial** division announced that a **government** order would make it **necessary** to **determine** more carefully the **quantity** of goods that could be listed in the **catalog**. Since the new **requirement** set **definite** limits, a **recommendation** was made that full **cooperation** be the **basis** for future action. In one **sense** the **existence** of the regulation gave the company an **excellent** chance to make its **acquaint-**

ance with those products that would **benefit** both the consumer and the seller. No one in good **conscience** would take the **authority** on this **occasion** to ignore the report, but would proceed to make the proper adjustments.

Write Words Incorrectly Spelled Below:

_____

_____

_____

_____

_____

Compose Paragraph After Study of Missed Words:

_____

_____

_____

_____

_____

NINTH WEEK: Monday
Word 41:   guard i an

Pronunciation: _____

Image: GUARDian

                  _____

                  _____

                  _____

Bond: The GUARDian will GUARD my in-
                  terests.

                  _____

                  _____

                  _____

Trace: _____*guardian*_____

                  _____

                  _____

                  _____

Sentences: **Guardian** rights were given to his uncle.
                  Refer this to the **guardian** for proper
                  action.
                  I think we ought to ask her **guardian.**

NINTH WEEK: Tuesday
Word 42:   du ly

Pronunciation: _____

Image: dULY

                _____

                _____

                _____

Bond: The note was dULY paid in JULY.

                _____

                _____

                _____

Trace: _____*duly*_____

                _____

                _____

                _____

Sentences: **Duly** signed statements were mailed.
                The message has **duly** arrived.
                The bill must be paid **duly**.

NINTH WEEK: Wednesday
Word 43: sov er eign

Pronunciation: _____

Image: soveREIGN

_____

_____

_____

Bond: The REIGN of the soveREIGN was short.

_____

_____

_____

Trace: *sovereign*

_____

_____

_____

Sentences: **Sovereign** rights were given the ruler.
He has been the **sovereign** for forty years.
The boy dreamed that one day he would be **sovereign**.

NINTH WEEK: Thursday
Word 44:   peas ant

Pronunciation: _____

Image: PEASant

           _____

           _____

           _____

Bond: A PEASant sometimes ate only PEAS.

           _____

           _____

           _____

Trace: *peasant*

           _____

           _____

           _____

Sentences: **Peasant** rights were simply unknown.

           It was the **peasant** who longed for a revolt.

           The salt tax was a heavy burden on the **peasant**.

NINTH WEEK: Friday

Word 45: ex traor di nar y

Pronunciation: _____

Image: EXTRAordinary

_____

_____

_____

Bond: EXTRAordinary means something EX-
TRA above ORDINARY.

_____

_____

_____

Trace: *extraordinary*

_____

_____

_____

Sentences: **Extraordinary** events were taking place.
It was an **extraordinary** exhibition of
skill.
It is nothing **extraordinary**.

Review: 10 Sentences on Saturday

_____

_____

_____

_____

_____

_____

_____

_____

_____

_____

5 Sentences on Sunday

_____

_____

_____

_____

_____

TENTH WEEK: Monday

Word 46: mon arch y

Pronunciation: _____

Image: monARCHy

_____

_____

_____

Bond: The ARCH was a symbol of the mon-
ARCHy.

_____

_____

_____

Trace: *monarchy*

_____

_____

_____

Sentences: A **monarchy** will not be established.

The aim of the **monarchy** was to create order.

The people voted against the **monarchy**.

TENTH WEEK: Tuesday
Word 47:   cor dial ly

Pronunciation: _____

Image: cordiALLY

_____

_____

_____

Bond: His ALLY replied cordiALLY.
See VI—the "LY" Ending

_____

_____

_____

Trace: _cordially_

_____

_____

_____

Sentences: **Cordially** was hardly the way he spoke.
They were **cordially** given answers.
Everyone was received **cordially**.

TENTH WEEK:	Wednesday
Word 48:	mir a cle
Pronunciation:	_____
Image:	mIRAcle
	_____
	_____
	_____
Bond:	IRA thought it was a mIRAcle.
	See V—Word Relatives
	_____
	_____
	_____
Trace:	_____ *miracle* _____
	_____
	_____
	_____

Sentences: "**Miracle** power" is an advertising slogan.
It seemed that a **miracle** was about to happen.
He would be saved only by a **miracle**.

TENTH WEEK: Thursday
Word 49:   clothes

Pronunciation: _____

Image: CLOTHes

_____

_____

_____

Bond: There is CLOTH in CLOTHes.

_____

_____

_____

Trace: *clothes*

_____

_____

_____

Sentences: **Clothes** make the man.
You will need warm **clothes** in this climate.
His business was to press **clothes**.

TENTH WEEK: Friday
Word 50: pri or

Pronunciation: _____

Image: pRIOr

_____

_____

_____

Bond: They stopped pRIOr to reaching the
RIO Grande.

_____

_____

_____

Trace: *prior*

_____

_____

_____

Sentences: **Prior** to his speech, the chairman asked
for applause.
It happened **prior** to my arrival.
I don't know whose rights are **prior**.

Review: 10 Sentences on Saturday

_____

_____

_____

_____

_____

_____

_____

_____

_____

_____

5 Sentences on Sunday

_____

_____

_____

_____

_____

ELEVENTH WEEK: Monday
Word 51:   com mit tee

Pronunciation: _____

Image: coMMiTTEE

       _____

       _____

       _____

Bond: Double MTE when you write coMMiT-
TEE.

       _____

       _____

       _____

Trace: *committee*

       _____

       _____

       _____

Sentences: **Committee** members must be present.
Give it to the **committee** for further ac-
tion.
Who is the head of the **committee?**

ELEVENTH WEEK: Tuesday
Word 52:   cour te sy

Pronunciation: _____

Image: COURTesy

                    _____

                    _____

                    _____

Bond: COURTesy was part of COURT man-
                    ners.

                    _____

                    _____

                    _____

Trace: _____ *courtesy* _____

                    _____

                    _____

                    _____

Sentences: Courtesy is a way of life.
                    An act of courtesy is always admired.
                    The children must be taught courtesy.

ELEVENTH WEEK: Wednesday
Word 53:   o rig i nal

Pronunciation: _____

Image: oriGINal

                  _____

                  _____

                  _____

Bond: It was a model of the oriGINal cotton
                  GIN.
                  See V—Word Relatives

                  _____

                  _____

                  _____

Trace: _____ *original* _____

                  _____

                  _____

                  _____

Sentences: **Original** drawings are valuable.
                  I want the **original** of that letter.
                  This painting doesn't look **original**.

ELEVENTH WEEK: Thursday

Word 54:   un doubt ed ly

Pronunciation: _____

Image: unDOUBTedly

     _____

     _____

     _____

Bond: He was unDOUBTedly without a
     DOUBT.

     _____

     _____

     _____

Trace: *undoubtedly*

     _____

     _____

     _____

Sentences: **Undoubtedly**, you are right.
     It was **undoubtedly** the work of a thief.
     It's the real thing—**undoubtedly!**

ELEVENTH WEEK: Friday
Word 55:   e di tion

Pronunciation: _____

Image: EDITion

Bond: I will EDIT this EDITion.

Trace: *edition*

Sentences: Edition after edition was sold out.
                    This is the edition I want.
                    He owns a first edition.

Review: 10 Sentences on Saturday

_____

_____

_____

_____

_____

_____

_____

_____

_____

_____

5 Sentences on Sunday

_____

_____

_____

_____

_____

TWELFTH WEEK: Monday
Word 56: op por tu ni ty

Pronunciation: _____

Image: opPORTunity

_____

_____

_____

Bond: Take the opPORTunity to visit the PORT.

_____

_____

_____

Trace: *opportunity*

_____

_____

_____

Sentences: **Opportunity** is supposed to knock once.
This is the **opportunity** I've wanted.
Give them every **opportunity**.

TWELFTH WEEK: Tuesday
Word 57: mur mur

Pronunciation: _____

Image: MUR MUR

_____

_____

_____

Bond: Say MUR twice and you MURMUR.

_____

_____

_____

Trace: *murmur*

_____

_____

_____

_____

Sentences: Murmur the word, but don't shout.
A strong murmur of approval was heard in the crowd.
It is more than a murmur.

TWELFTH WEEK: Wednesday
Word 58:   ac cept a ble

Pronunciation: _____

Image: ACCEPTable

                  _____

                  _____

                  _____

Bond: If it is ACCEPTABLE, you are ABLE
                  to ACCEPT.
                  See VI—The "ABLE-IBLE" Ending

                  _____

                  _____

                  _____

Trace: *acceptable*

                  _____

                  _____

                  _____

Sentences: **Acceptable** reasons were given.
                  It is not **acceptable** to all.
                  Make sure the amount is **acceptable**.

TWELFTH WEEK: Thursday

Word 59:   bear ing

Pronunciation: _____

Image: BEARing

        _____

        _____

        _____

Bond: ℩He was BEARing a BEAR on his back.

        _____

        _____

        _____

Trace: *bearing*

        _____

        _____

        _____

Sentences: **Bearing** to his left, he came upon the house.

        This has no **bearing** on the case.

        The car has a burned out **bearing**.

TWELFTH WEEK: Friday
Word 60:   fare well

Pronunciation: _____

Image: FAREwell

  _____

  _____

  _____

Bond: He waved FAREwell after paying his FARE.

  _____

  _____

Trace: *farewell*

  _____

  _____

  _____

Sentences: **Farewell** was said in short order.
He bade **farewell** to his men.
Let me offer you a fond **farewell**.

Review: 15 Sentences on Saturday

_____

_____

_____

_____

_____

_____

_____

1 Paragraph (next page)
Sunday Morning

_____

_____

_____

1 Paragraph Sunday Evening

_____

_____

_____

_____

Review Paragraphs: Third Month

When you have done these paragraphs you have completed your ninety day trial. You ought to feel better about spelling now. A word is no longer your boss. You've changed places. Don't stop here. Get after other words that bother you.

The first paragraph below covers 41-60. The second reviews a selected list from the 1-40 group. Any time you want to check yourself on all sixty, just turn to the "Advanced List" in the Appendix.

I.

The second **edition** of the book included an **extraordinary** tale of Beppo, a poor farmer who had been secretly appointed **guardian** of a boy who would some day be **sovereign** of the land. At the time, a **committee** of court officials had been ruling the **monarchy,** and the leader **undoubtedly** had hopes that he could be made so **acceptable** that the **original** prince would never be **duly** crowned. However, despite his shabby **clothes,** the lowly field worker decided to go to the palace. He bade **farewell** to his young charge, and promised that only a **miracle** would destroy the **opportunity** to become king.

Beppo arrived just **prior** to a move that had been planned to seize the throne. Of course, he was not **cordially** greeted, but his fine **courtesy** and dignified **bearing** caused a **murmur** of protest to be raised against his dismissal. The proof that the real prince was alive brought great joy to the people. Thus did a **peasant** save a king.

II.

That television has become a **permanent** part of **American** life is a definite fact. Despite the criticism that has been raised on occasion, every authority in the field agrees that more benefit than harm will eventually occur. It is true the exhausted viewer has not yet learned to use his judgment in selecting the excellent programs over those that merely interrupt his normal activities. Nevertheless, as the novelty wears off, it will become necessary for the studio executive to ascertain whether quantity can take the place of quality. Certainly greater acquaintance with this form of entertainment will improve public taste. Then, if only for financial reasons, a recommendation for good presentations will be possible. People of good sense will decide that junk doesn't warrant their attention.

Write Words Incorrectly Spelled Below:

_____

_____

_____

Compose Paragraph After Study of Missed Words:

_____

_____

_____

· IX ·

General Program

You've proved to yourself that you too can be a good speller. But please don't get smug about it. There are probably a number of common words that still need study. Moreover, you will occasionally meet new words to master. But from here on you are on your own. All you need is a long-range plan. We will give you a ten step program, but only *you* can put it into action.

1. Get a looseleaf notebook. Divide it into three sections. Reserve the first section for any word you use frequently and misspell almost always. Arrange the words as was done in the "Ninety Day Trial." Give each entry THE TREATMENT.

    Label the middle pages "Rarely Used—Like to Know." These will be words you hear now and then, but are not the bread and butter of your daily language diet. Save them for a time when you can be selective about adding to your stock.

    In the final section list the words you have mastered. Set them up in groups of ten under the heading "Mastered List." When you have accumulated this number, compose a paragraph—a story, description, anything—using the former demons. Occasionally ask someone to dictate what you have written so that you can test yourself. Any time you misspell a word in this section, put it back to the beginning, and start all over again with it. Any error shows that you haven't established the correct habit yet.

2. Take your time. Never handle more than **one word a day.** Remember also that a few minutes at a time spread over three periods of the day are far better than six minutes spent all at once. That's worth repeating: 3 minutes in the morning, 1½ in the afternoon, and 1½ in the evening—SIX MINUTES A DAY ARE ALL YOU NEED TO MASTER ANY WORD.

3. Practice writing words **without stopping in the middle for any reason.** Trust your hand. If you have the right habit, you will spell the word right. If not, put the word in section I of your notebook, and give it THE TREATMENT. That old saying applies perfectly to spelling: "He who hesitates is lost."

4. Write legibly. Don't worry about the beautiful kind of handwriting few of us can imitate. But if you want to write an E, let there be no doubt it is an E. Every letter should be clear. Mechanical accuracy will increase your confidence.

5. After you complete any piece of writing, re-read it with care, even if it is a note dashed off in pencil. So-called typographical errors are errors just the same.

6. Once you master a word, use it often. This will help you practice. And you will prove to yourself that you are no longer afraid of misspelling.

7. If you find crossword puzzles amusing, by all means work them. You probably rarely remember a new word from them, but they do offer good spelling review. Word building games can be helpful, too.

8. When you listen to the radio, or watch television, keep a pad nearby. Write some of the words you hear, especially those you've had trouble spelling before. DO THIS AS YOU LISTEN! If you can write the words correctly while you are concentrating on a program, they are yours for a lifetime.

9. Watch your speech. If someone says a word differently from the way you pronounce it, look it up. Remember the case of Mr. D, the man with the automobile accessories stores? His spoken mistakes came to roost in his writing.

10. Don't quit! You may be full of fight for a few weeks. Then you may get that let-down feeling. Don't give in. You can do this job easily, quickly—if you get stubborn about it.

•   •   •

Incidentally, learning to spell properly isn't all drudgery. You can have fun with words, too. The next four chapters will talk about some of the interesting facts in the background of modern spelling. They will show you how to trace word histories, will give you a few amusing examples of mistakes careless spellers make, and will introduce a *new spelling game*.

Each chapter is not intended as the final word on the subject it outlines. You should, however, be able to use the material as suggestions for further investigation on your own. You will improve your spelling and enjoy many hours of pleasant reading.

Tittle Page

A Handefull
of pleasant delites

Containing sundrie new sonets
and delectable histories, in
divers kindes of Meeter.

Newly devised to the newest tunes
that are now in use, to be sung:
everie Sonet orderly pointed
to his proper Tune.

With new additions of certain Songs,
to verie late devised Notes not
Commonly Knowen, not
used heretofore.

By Clement Robinson
and divers others

AT LONDON

Printed by Richard Lhones: dwel-
ling at the signe of the Rose
and Crowne, neare
Holburne Bridge
1584

X

Spelling Long Ago

To the left is what an old song sheet published over three hundred and fifty years ago looked like. Can you find the 14 misspellings, according to today's standards? Notice the strange use of capital letters. You may well wonder how the printer kept his job.

In fact, Mr. Lhones was simply spelling as he pleased. But there were no accepted authorities then, and each writer or printer was free to be his own dictionary. For instance, you could even beat Shakespeare in a modern spelling bee. Here is the first page of his greatest play. What 14 words would Miss Kitteridge at Billboard High School mark wrong?

"The Tragicall Historie of

HAMLET

Prince of Denmarke

Enter two Centinels (now called Bernardo & Francisco)

1. Stand: who is that?
2. Tis I.
1. O you come most carefully upon your watch,
2. And if you meete Marcellus and Horatio
   The partners of my watch, bid them make haste.
1. I will: See who goes there.

Hor. Friends to this ground
Mar. And leegemen to the Dane
    O farewell honest souldier, who hath releeved
    you?
1. Bernardo hath my place, give you good night
Mar. Holla, Bernardo
2. Say, is Horatio there?
Hor. A peece of him.
2. Welcome Horatio, welcome good Marcellus.
Mar. What hath this thing appear'd againe tonight.
2. I have seene nothing.
Mar. Horatio sayes tis but our fantasie,
    And wil not let beliefe take hold of him,
    Touching this dreaded sight twice seene by
    us, . . ."

Even the great John Milton, author of "Paradise Lost," would be given the dunce cap in an eighth grade English class today. This selection from a poem on his twenty-third birthday is full of errors in spelling, punctuation, and capitalization—according to the way we would write.

"How soone hath Time the suttle theefe of Youth
    Stolne on his wing my three & twentith yeere
    my hasting days fly on with full careere
    but my late spring no bud or blossome shew'th

Perhapps my semblance might deceave ye truth
    that I to manhood am arriv'd so neere
    & inward ripenesse doth much lesse appeare
    that some more tymely-happie spirits indu'th"

Before you start saying, "What was good enough for the masters is good enough for me," you must realize that it was only because the writers themselves began to try for some sort of regularity that modern spelling emerged. They recognized the eventual confusion that would result from spelling by ear. By the eighteenth century, great progress toward uniformity had been made. In one of the first magazines ever published, "The Spectator," edited by Joseph Addison and Richard Steele, we can see fewer differences from our style of writing than existed during the reign of the first Elizabeth.

> "   Thursday, March 1, 1711
>
>   . . . . I had not been long at the University before I distinguished myself by a most profound Silence. For during the Space of eight Years, excepting in the publick Exercises of the College, I scarce uttered the Quantity of an hundred Words; and indeed do not remember that I ever spoke three Sentences together in my whole Life . . ."

By the time Boswell had stopped recording the life of Dr. Johnson in the latter half of the eighteenth century, a page of a London manuscript would have shown few surprises to us.

Oddly enough, however, we Americans took longer to straighten out our letters and punctuation marks. That is partly why some experts claim that our version of English is actually older in form than the modern British.

Less than two hundred years ago, when England was beginning to standardize its spelling, our forefathers were still spelling by ear. In this selection from a charming story about a trip to New York from Boston, Sarah Kemble Knight would have fitted in nicely with English writers who lived a hundred years before her.

"I was Interogated by . . . the Eldest daughter of the family, with these . . . . words, (viz.) 'Law for mee-what in the world brings You here at this time a night?—I never see a woman on the Rode so Dreadfull late, in all the days of my versall life. Who are You? Where are you going? I'me scar'd out of my witts' . . . . when in comes my Guide-to him Madam turn'd Roreing out: 'Lawfull heart, John, is it You?—how de do! Where in the world are you going with this woman? Who is she?' "

You will agree that loose spelling is interesting, and certainly colorful. But failure to use agreed-upon spellings eventually would have led in writing to what happened in nations where dialects became too widespread and numerous. It is not unusual for some countrymen to speak the same basic language, but fail to understand one another because of the difference in dialect. Be glad that *you* can point to any word and say,

"This is how it should be spelled!"

XI

Spelling and the Family Tree

Tracing words to their original sources can be fascinating. There are many interesting stories behind modern usage. But apart from the entertainment you can have learning the history of a particular word family, you can also gain valuable aid in your spelling problems.

For example, in the days of the Romans, when a man was an officeseeker he was required to wear a white toga or robe to let the people know that he was anxious for their votes. CANDIDUS is the Latin term for "robed in white." Hence we have the present use of the word CANDIDATE for one who is trying to be elected.

Knowing this fact can help you establish a bond with the difficult part of the word, in this case the DID syllable. Thus, while a good association is always useful, an enriched understanding of the meaning is so much the better.

Here are some additional derivations that make good reading as well as strong bonds. Get into the habit of checking the family tree of every word you look up. It might sound silly if you told someone you spent a few hours "reading" the dictionary. But in fact it can be as much fun as a novel.

ABUNDANCE. This is also from the Latin AB (from) and UNDA (wave). Since water is very plentiful, anything appearing in wave-like quantities would be abundant. Note the A in UNDA as a bond for **Ance.**

ADJECTIVE. Here it is AD (toward, at) and JACERE (to throw). These words are literally thrown at others (nouns) to make them clearer or more colorful. The DJ combination stands out this way, doesn't it?

ALPHABET. The first two letters in Greek are ALPHA and BETA. The word therefore means nothing more than the "A, B's." Note the PH in ALPHA for your spelling aid.

BARBAROUS. The Greeks thought any language other than their own crude, rough, uncivilized. They referred to strange foreign sounds as BAR-BAR, nonsense sounds. Note how the first two syllables of the word are merely repeats, thus helping you remember the two A's.

BOYCOTT. Captain Boycott was an agent for an Irish landlord whose rents were very high. The collector was subjected to social isolation as a protest by the people. Somehow we seem to remember the spelling of a name more readily than some words so that perhaps you will not forget to use the double T when you write BOYCOTT.

CHAUVINISM. Nicholas Chauvin was a member of Napoleon's army, and he was so intensely patriotic that gradually he became a joke among his associates. Spelling the name right helps you over the major hurdle in the word.

DAHLIA. The Swedish botanist, DAHL, had this flower named after him. Don't leave that H out!

DISASTROUS. We go back to Latin for DIS (against)

and ASTRA (stars); anything happening contrary to the stars, or good fortune, would be DISASTROUS. Note the TR combination in ASTRA. Don't put any letter between the two when you write the word.

DUFFEL. This came from a town in England where a type of rough woollen cloth was made. Today the duffel bag is made of canvas, but the spelling of the town is still with us.

EXHILARATE. Again we are in ancient Rome where we meet EX (out of) and HILARIS (cheerful); anything that produces a good feeling **exhilarates.** Note the LAR, and keep the A there.

EXORBITANT. This really means "out of the orbit," or unusually above the average. Start with EX, add ORBIT, and there you are.

INNUENDO. IN (toward) plus NUERE (to nod) combine to give us a word that applies to a statement that doesn't make its point directly but sort of nods in the right direction. You can see where we get the two N's.

LISTERINE. It was easy for this product to take the name of the English scientist, Lord Lister, and make a word out of it.

LUNATIC. You can remember the A in this word by recalling that it comes from LUNA (the moon). An old superstition claimed that one who stared at the moon would go mad.

MACADAM. The Scottish engineer who thought of a new road-surfacing material lent his name to the product.

MAUSOLEUM. In 353 B.C. the wife of King Mausolus ordered a magnificent monument erected in his memory. Start with the name and the rest is easy.

MESMERIZE. F. A. Mesmer, an Austrian doctor and hypnotist, found his name attached to the technique of causing people to fall asleep or lose their wills. The name itself isn't hard at all.

NICOTINE. Jacques Nicot, the French ambassador at Lisbon, sent some plants back to one of the DeMedicis. Judging from modern advertising, he didn't do us a favor because he's the one (at least in the word) we try to get rid of. Note the OT.

PANDEMONIUM. When a home run is hit and pandemonium reigns, the place is really full (pan) of demons (demonium). Put the demon in the middle and you chase his spelling friends away.

QUARANTINE. Formerly, when a person had a communicable disease, he was required to stay indoors for 40 (quaranta) days. Today the period is shorter, but the ARA combination has not changed.

SACRILEGE. Some shady customers used to like to collect (legere) sacred (sacri) objects. The trouble was that they didn't bother to ask anyone's permission, and now SACRILEGE, with the E from LEG, implies an act or statement against religious beliefs.

VULCANIZE. The Norse god VULCAN would forge and hammer weapons for his fellow inhabitants of the clouds. Now he has been reduced to a tire patch.

WORSTED. This is just the name of an English town, and the R is a typical silent British letter.

ZINNIA. The German botanist, J. G. Zinn, has been immortalized by this lovely flower. Note the double N.

Of course, these twenty-five are but a handful of the thousands of word histories waiting for you to uncover their mysteries. And more often than not, the illogical modern spelling is the result of the odd names and language combinations that were taken bodily into our collection. This is one more time that you can look to the ancestors for the faults in the descendants.

If You Want to Read More:

Highly entertaining style, brief little stories, charming illustrations:

In A Word—Margaret S. Ernst, James Thurber. (Knopf)
Word Histories— Wendell Herbruck. (Dorset)

Extensive coverage, very scholarly, literally stuffed with language lore:

Thereby Hangs a Tale—C. E. Funk. (Harper)
The American Language—H. L. Mencken. (Knopf)
The Loom of Language—F. Bodmer. (Norton)

XII

Spelling Boners

Ordinarily, when you've been guilty of a misspelling, there is nothing to laugh about. You are seriously concerned about the word, and you should add it to the list that forms your personal study program. However, now and then you may discover that the error has resulted in a rather amusing sentence, especially when the wrong form suggests another word that changes the meaning entirely.

You ought to enjoy these taken from examination papers, newspaper columns, letters, reports, and similar materials. After you've had a chuckle or two, consider how easily all the mistakes, frequently the result of only carelessness, could have been eliminated simply by a more careful re-reading before release to the reader.

Watch out for these "boners." Check what you write. If you find something to laugh about in your work, have a good time, and then get rid of it before anyone else sees it. Here are some samples. In the second sentence the word is used correctly.

·   ·   ·

Paul was visibly **infected** by her words.
She wasn't the least **affected** by his, however.

·   ·   ·

The cab driver was **carousing** all over town looking for a fare.

And a police car was **cruising** around looking for him.

* * *

He was a **stench** upholder of fair play.

So **staunch** a principle should not be suppressed.

* * *

The Arabs had nothing but the **dessert** to live on, so they didn't have enough to eat.

What else can one grow on a **desert**?

* * *

Louis XVI was **gelatined** by the Jacobins.

After he was **guillotined**, of course!

* * *

His signature was so **eligible** that the bank refused to cash his check.

Besides, his handwriting was **illegible**!

* * *

She was **tide** up all morning.

And she came out cleaner than any soap, with one hand **tied** behind her back.

* * *

Many of our colonies were founded by people who had been **executed**.

Afterwards, they were **exiled**.

* * *

Salt Lake City is a place where the **Morons** settled.

The **Mormons** weren't too happy about them.

* * *

Some southern families employed **tooters** for their children.
Could the **tutor** play the tooter?

.   .   .

Typhoid fever can be prevented by **fascination**.
Vaccination is equally helpful.

.   .   .

They recommended that I read "The Queen's **Neckless**."
I never did find out how she could wear a **necklace**.

.   .   .

When I buy things, money is no **objection**.
But my **object** is to keep the price down.

.   .   .

My mother is what most people would call a **warrior**.
Poor papa is the **worrier**.

.   .   .

He graduated **semi** cum laude.
If he had doubled his marks, he might have made **summa**
cum laude.

.   .   .

I hope that some **sore** of truce will come in the future.
This **sort** of thing leads to wars.

.   .   .

George ate a lonely meal in the **dinning** room.
His ear plugs made **dining** possible.

.   .   .

Mr. Kent's favorite meal was stake smothered in unions.
On the other hand, the president of the local preferred steak with onions.

．　　　．　　　．

The batter hit a fowl that went clear out of the park.
I'll bet he suspected foul play.

．　　　．　　　．

Beginning of a letter: "Dear Anut Sally,"
Really, frankness can go just so far, even with an aunt!

．　　　．　　　．

It was just to make sure that no one would enroach on his territory.
Nor did he want to encroach on theirs.

．　　　．　　　．

· XIII ·

Spellagrams

You have probably tried your hand at crossword puzzles, anagrams, cryptograms, and other word games. However, most of these are not very helpful for sharpening spelling habits. Either there is too much to do, or sufficient stress is not laid on letter combinations directly.

This new game, the SPELLAGRAM, has been designed to be of value *especially* to those who have spelling problems. Once you have gotten the general idea, you'll find it both instructive and fun. You can make the SPELLAGRAM a fascinating parlor game. We'll tell you how later. And, by the way, there are three forms! When you tire of one, play another. Here are the rules.

Spellagram — Form A

N E C I N E C O S C   D R O B I F S

‾ ‾ ‾ ‾ ‾ ‾ ‾ ‾ ‾ ‾   ‾ ‾ ‾ ‾ ‾ ‾ ‾

(one's inner self)   (prohibits)

C L A S P I E   G R E E L I V I S P

‾ ‾ ‾ ‾ ‾ ‾ ‾   ‾ ‾ ‾ ‾ ‾ ‾ ‾ ‾ ‾

(particular)   (favors, advantages)

Rules

1. The four blanks represent words which when worked out will read like a telegram message. Each space in the blank is for one letter.

2. Above the blank is the word that belongs in the spaces, but it is in scrambled form.

3. Below the blank is the definition of the word. This is to give you a hint.

4. Your job is simply to use the meanings to help you unscramble the words so that the message reads correctly. In this case, you would finally arrive at CONSCIENCE FORBIDS SPECIAL PRIVILEGES.

5. Note that *every letter in the scrambled word must be used*. Cross each one out as you place it in its proper space.

6. If you have used all the letters, but in the wrong order, you are charged with a misspelling.

7. The scoring is easy. Count the letters in the word missed, and subtract the sum from the total number of letters in the message. For example, this one has 34 letters in all. If you had missed PRIVILEGES, you would take 10 from 34, leaving you with the final score of 24.

Spellagram — Form B

This is the second form of the game.

8

– – – – – – – –
(set apart)

8

– – – – – – – –
(accommodations)

9

– – – – – – – – –
(usable, at hand)

11

– – – – – – – – – – –
(at once, now)

```
A A A A A A A    I I I    Q        U
B                L L L    R R R    V
D                M M      S S      Y
E E E E E E      P        T T T
```

Rules

1. The number above the blank indicates how many letters there are in the word.

2. As in Form A, the definitions below the blanks are hints about the words needed to complete the message.

3. Below the puzzle are listed the letters to be used in filling in the spaces.

4. When you have decided on a word, cross out the letters required to write it, and put the word in the blank.

5. Do this until you have completed the message.

6. Naturally, if you have misspelled any words, you will find a shortage of some letters, or too many of others. Thus you will be forced to check your work. Remember; ALL LETTERS MUST HAVE BEEN CROSSED OUT WHEN YOU HAVE FINISHED.

7. Here, too, you score by deducting the number of letters of each wrong word from the grand total. For example, this message is: SEPARATE QUARTERS AVAILABLE IMMEDIATELY, 36 letters in all. If you misspelled SEPARATE, your score is 36 less 8, or 28.

You can form teams among your friends. Each side makes up the SPELLAGRAMS for the other, or a neutral party does the work for both sides. Here's how you keep score:

1. In any series or round, the SPELLAGRAM for both sides must have the same number of letters.

2. Time the period it takes each team to work out the SPELLAGRAM.

3. Make the usual deductions for errors in spelling as outlined above.

4. Add the difference in time it takes one group to finish as compared to the other.

5. Suppose Team A finishes the puzzle accurately in 3 minutes, and Team B in 5 minutes. In a 36 letter game, the final score would be 38-36 in favor of A. Of course, misspellings would further affect the score.

Spellagram — Form C

1. The basic game takes two players. Each player has a pad of paper and a pencil. Also one of the players should have a watch. The player to go first is chosen by the flip of a coin or the drawing of a card.

2. Player A, the first player, selects a word. He then records the word on one slip of paper (out of sight of his opponent) and on another slip of paper he writes the word in scrambled form.

3. At the word "Go!" player A gives the scrambled word to player B.

4. Player B has two minutes to work out the word. If he manages to get the original word, he gets the full number of points corresponding to the number of letters. If he gets another word but still uses up all the letters of the scrambled word, he gets credit for the number of letters minus 1. If he cannot discover a word that uses all the letters, he tries to make any word or words he can, with as many letters as he can. He then gets credit for the number of letters used. But any misspellings mean a zero score for the round.

5. Player B now composes his word, and gives it in scrambled form to A. However, he must use *the same number of letters* player A used.

6. The player who has the highest score at the end of each round has the advantage of leading off

the next round. If the players are tied, the advantage remains with the same player until his opponent has a higher score.

7. Score is kept on the basis of points, and the player who arrives at 100 or more points first wins the game.

8. The game can also be played by four people, two against two, with partners working on the scrambled words.

Here is the start of a sample game:

1. Player A wins the toss.

2. He now selects SMATTER (7 letters) as his word. He writes SMATTER on one piece of paper and on another he writes RASETMT (a scrambled form of SMATTER).

3. At the word "Go!" A gives B the slip of paper with the scrambled word form, and B now has two minutes to unscramble the word.

4. If, within two minutes, B gets SMATTER he is credited with 7 full points (one for each letter in the original word). If he chooses MATTERS, he gets 6 points. (He has used all the letters but has not guessed the right word!) If he gets MASTER he gets 6 points. (There is still one T left over.) If he can think of only MATE or MAST he gets only 4 points. If he misspells, he gets 0 points.

5. It is now B's turn to give a word to A. B chooses COLLEGE (another 7 letter word) and passes on GLELEOC to A who has two minutes to see what he can do with that patchwork of letters. And so the game progresses. Remember: the next words can be ten letters or eight letters or any number just so that in each round the opponents use words of the same length.

Here are some additional Spellagrams for Forms A and B:

Additional Spellagrams—Form A

1)
NOVEMTNERG

_ _ _ _ _ _ _ _ _ _
(rule)

CANTREMINOMODE

_ _ _ _ _ _ _ _ _ _ _ _ _
(statement favoring)

TUBELDOYNDU

_ _ _ _ _ _ _ _ _ _
(unquestionably)

PACLABEECT

_ _ _ _ _ _ _ _ _
(welcome)

2)
DENENTRUSPENIT

_ _ _ _ _ _ _ _ _ _ _ _
(person in charge)

PLIGELENX

_ _ _ _ _ _ _ _
(ejecting)

COMESHISUVI

_ _ _ _ _ _ _ _ _ _
(full of tricks)

TRIMYOORD

_ _ _ _ _ _ _ _
(rooms in college)

SPUTACONC

_ _ _ _ _ _ _ _ _
(dwellers)

3)

ETOOBULAIM

_ _ _ _ _ _ _ _ _
(four-wheeled car)

TIXBIHE

_ _ _ _ _ _ _
(show)

NIGENBING

_ _ _ _ _ _ _ _
(starting)

DEWSNEADY

_ _ _ _ _ _ _ _ _
(fourth day)

GOTINCINUN

_ _ _ _ _ _ _ _ _
(lasting)

GRASTHIT

_ _ _ _ _ _ _ _
(not bent)

HOGHURT

_ _ _ _ _ _ _
(end to end)

YARRBUEF

_ _ _ _ _ _ _ _
(very cold one)

Spellagrams—Form B

1)

9

_ _ _ _ _ _ _ _ _
(chosen group)

11

_ _ _ _ _ _ _ _ _ _ _
(assuredly)

7

_ _ _ _ _ _ _
(looks for)

8

_ _ _ _ _ _ _
(full)

10

_ _ _ _ _ _ _ _ _ _
(being present)

A A A A	F	N N N	T T T T T T
C C C C C C	I I I	O O	X
D D	L	P P	Y Y
E E E E E E E	M M	S	

2)

8

_ _ _ _ _ _
(trade)

5

_ _ _ _ _
(time measure)

10

_ _ _ _ _ _ _ _ _
(kept running)

7

_ _ _ _ _ _ _
(notwithstanding)

6

_ _ _ _ _ _
(every 365 days)

11

_ _ _ _ _ _ _ _ _ _ _
(holiday observance)

```
A A A A A  E E E E E E  M              R R
B B        H            N N N N N N    S S S S S
C          I I I I I    O O            T T T
D D        L L          P              U U U
```

3)

7

_ _ _ _ _ _ _
(not native)

14

_ _ _ _ _ _ _ _ _ _ _ _ _ _
(delegates)

9

_ _ _ _ _ _ _ _ _
(warmly)

8

_ _ _ _ _ _ _ _
(presenting)

9

_ _ _ _ _ _ _ _ _
(very good)

9

_ _ _ _ _ _ _ _ _
(of money)

11

_ _ _ _ _ _ _ _ _ _ _
(working together)

AAAAA	FFFF	NNNNNNN	S
CCCC	GG	OOOOOO	TTTT
D	IIIIII	PP	V
EEEEEEEEEE	LLLLL	RRRRR	X
			Y

ANSWERS

Form A—1) Government recommendation undoubtedly acceptable.

2) Superintendent expelling mischievous dormitory occupants.

3) Automobile exhibit beginning Wednesday continuing straight through February.

Form B—1) Committee confidently expects capacity attendance.

2) Business hours maintained despite annual celebration.

3) Foreign representative cordially offering excellent financial cooperation.

Appendix

This section contains 2500 selected words. You will note that they have been divided into three groups—basic (including "100 Spelling Demons"), average, and advanced. This has been done to enable you to find out for yourself just where you fit in terms of general ability.

If you can spell all in the basic list, you are doing about as well as a person with an elementary school background. A score of 100% in the average group indicates that you can hold your own with most people, regardless of their educational training. After you have achieved complete accuracy with the advanced words, you will be able to call yourself a superior speller.

Go through each list systematically. Have someone dictate the trial sentences to you, or look at them rapidly and write them from memory. As soon as you have accumulated twenty words that require further study, take one a day for a month as described in the "Ninety Day Trial." Test the results of your planned attack, and if you make no mistakes, go on to the next group of sentences. In general, then, it is TEST, STUDY, TEST.

One final word. We've said it before. It must be said again. DON'T QUIT! The rewards for your efforts to improve your spelling will be very worthwhile. You will write with confidence. You will avoid frequent embarrassment. Best of all, you will gradually add new words to your vocabulary because you will no longer fear their spelling.

Basic List

100 Spelling Demons
Sentences

1-25

1. We can't choose the blue color again.
2. The country doctor is always busy among his people.
3. I believe this business is dear to him because he built it from the beginning.
4. If the cough does make your chest ache, buy something to break it up.
5. There could not have been any answer to why he was coming.

26-50

1. Learn grammar early enough and you will find it easy to know what is correct.
2. I heard a hoarse voice and knew that my friend was here.
3. Instead of trying to guess, just try to hear every word.
4. The digging done, he laid the bulbs in loose soil, and watered them for half an hour.
5. Don't lose sight of the fact that they are having forty people to dinner in February.

Basic List

100 Spelling Demons

Words

ache	done
again	don't
always	early
among	easy
answer	enough
any	every
been	February
beginning	forty
believe	friend
blue	grammar
break	guess
built	half
business	having
busy	hear
buy	heard
can't	here
choose	hoarse
color	hour
coming	instead
cough	just
could	knew
country	know
dear	laid
doctor	loose
does	lose

Basic List Continued

100 Spelling Demons

Sentences

51-75

1. It seems that children can tear their new shoes in a minute.
2. There is a separate piece of sugar ready for your tea.
3. Some said the raise was sure to come at once.
4. He often says he meant to read it many times.
5. Making a straight line was much harder since none of them had a ruler.

76-100

1. Each week, on Tuesday and Wednesday, the women sell used things.
2. Though very tired, I'm writing tonight.
3. They wrote to ask whether the two boys would come.
4. I am truly too busy to write about the dress which I will wear.
5. There won't be any trouble if it is sent through the store where the whole record is kept.

Basic List Continued

100 Spelling Demons

Words

making	they
many	though
meant	through
minute	tired
much	tonight
none	too
often	trouble
once	truly
piece	Tuesday
raise	two
read	used
ready	very
said	wear
says	Wednesday
seems	week
separate	where
shoes	whether
since	which
some	whole
straight	women
sugar	won't
sure	would
tear	write
their	writing
there	wrote

Basic List Continued
Sentences
101-125

1. Struck by the **automobile**, the **angry** **animal** ran **across** the **avenue**.
2. The **advertisement** gave the **amount** of salary and the **address** where those **already** eighteen could **apply**.
3. Since the **accident**, the poor boy has been **absent**, and pays **almost** no **attention** to the **alphabet**.
4. **Although** he may not be **around** before late **August** or early **autumn**, we can **appoint** him **anyway**.
5. At the **army** post last **April**, my **aunt** slipped on a **banana** peel and fell **against** a wall.

126-150

1. The **butcher** sold a **certain** kind of **chicken** at a **cheap** price to **build** up his **trade**.
2. My **brother** took the **chalk** at the **blackboard** and drew a man with a **beautiful** **beard**.
3. Be **careful** to put the **candle** near the **chair** away from the **bottom** of the **Christmas** tree.
4. The **chief** scout put the **cheese** and a **bottle** of wine on a **board** **between** the weary travelers.
5. **Change** the **button** **because** it will rub your **cheek** if you are **careless**.

151-175

1. The **death** of the **conductor** in **December** caused the **company** to **close** the tour.
2. A good **citizen** knows the **danger** **cities** face when they fail to **collect** **court** fines.
3. The tired **dentist** poured **cream** into his **coffee**, ate a **cracker**, and then lit a **cigarette**.

Basic List Continued

4. We must **decide** on a **correct collar** for the **cotton** dress or the **customer** will not buy it.

5. Her **daughter** went to **church** to help her **cousin count** the **copies** of the new prayer books.

Words

absent	beard	church
accident	beautiful	cigarette
across	because	cities
address	between	citizen
advertisement	blackboard	close
against	board	coffee
almost	bottle	collar
alphabet	bottom	collect
already	brother	company
although	build	conductor
amount	butcher	copies
angry	button	correct
animal	candle	cotton
apply	careful	count
appoint	careless	court
April	certain	cousin
army	chair	cracker
around	chalk	cream
attention	change	customer
August	cheap	danger
aunt	cheek	daughter
automobile	cheese	death
autumn	chicken	December
avenue	chief	decide
banana	Christmas	dentist

Basic List Continued

176-200

1. We expect to pay a dollar and eighty cents for dinner this evening.
2. There are eight different parts to each exercise except the eleventh.
3. Eighteen people came to examine the empty houses and a dozen left a deposit.
4. Two men died some distance from the entrance to the factory when a mound of earth fell on them.
5. Either his education in English during the eighth year had been poor or he had forgotten everything.

201-225

1. I am looking forward to using the fourth Friday as a happy holiday.
2. Her husband planted the flower in the garden to avoid a family fight.
3. The hospital announced that the grocery clerk had been hit on the forehead with a heavy object like a hammer.
4. If they are hungry, fifteen grown boys can eat a gallon of ice cream in fourteen seconds.
5. The initials on the handkerchief were a great help in proving the forger had used a foreign name to pass a hundred bad checks.

226-250

1. June began to learn to laugh a little in kindergarten.
2. They will marry in January or March, and there is much interest in the match.
3. The length of the language lesson does not matter, so long as you listen.
4. It is known that a loaf of bread from the home kitchen will supply a good measure of iron.
5. Writing a letter in the light of a lazy July day will knock any idea of labor out of your mind.

Basic List Continued

deposit	family	interest
died	fifteen	iron
different	fight	January
dinner	flower	July
distance	forehead	June
dollar	foreign	kindergarten
dozen	forger	kitchen
earth	forward	knock
education	fourteen	known
eight	fourth	labor
eighteen	Friday	language
eighth	gallon	laugh
eighty	garden	learn
either	great	length
eleventh	grocery	lesson
empty	grown	letter
English	hammer	light
entrance	handkerchief	listen
evening	happy	little
everything	heavy	loaf
examine	holiday	March
except	hospital	marry
exercise	hundred	match
expect	hungry	matter
factory	husband	measure

Basic List Continued

251-275

1. **Neither** my **niece** nor her **mother** thought the new **mustache** suited my **nephew.**
2. **Monday morning** the **newspaper** announced that **nineteen** men had scaled the **mountain.**
3. All **month** he kept the **medicine near** his bed because he would **need** it in the **middle** of the **night.**
4. Even if he didn't invest another **nickel,** his **money** would soon **multiply** into **ninety million** dollars.
5. It **might** be a bad **mistake** to put a **needle** or a **nail** into your **mouth.**

276-300

1. A **perfect picture** of an **orange, peach,** and **pear** won the **prize.**
2. From **October** to **November,** the company **ought** to **offer** reduced rates for the **ocean** trip.
3. **People** of that **period** could buy a **pencil** and **paper** for a **penny.**
4. **Nothing** was heard until two **o'clock** of the **ninth** day, when **noise** in the streets told us **peace** had come.
5. Wearing his **overalls** under his **overcoat,** he brought an **ounce** or two of milk in a **pail** to ease the **pain** of the sick calf.

301-325

1. The **prime** reason for his **quest** was to **receive** a **promise** from the king.
2. Do everything in your **power** to keep him **quiet,** and **please remember** to put a **pillow** under his head.
3. In a talk lasting a **quarter** of an hour, the **president** found time to **refer** to the low pay of the **postman** and **policeman.**

Basic List Continued

4. It is **possible** the **prescription** slipped from my **pocket** when I took a **quick** trip to the **post office**.

5. In the **restaurant**, the **pretty** girl had some meat with a **plain** boiled **potato**, and then drank half a **quart** of milk.

medicine	ninth	pillow
middle	noise	plain
might	nothing	please
million	November	pocket
mistake	ocean	policeman
Monday	o'clock	possible
money	October	postman
month	offer	post office
morning	orange	potato
mother	ought	power
mountain	ounce	prescription
mouth	overalls	president
multiply	overcoat	pretty
mustache	pail	prime
nail	pain	promise
near	paper	quart
needle	peace	quarter
neither	peach	quest
nephew	pear	quick
newspaper	pencil	quiet
nickel	penny	reason
niece	people	receive
night	perfect	refer
nineteen	period	remember
ninety	picture	restaurant

Basic List Continued
326-350

1. The sight of silver paper and colored ribbon made sister think of Santa Claus.
2. They sail on the sixth of September and should arrive in seventeen days.
3. Although he called over his shoulder for a sandwich several times, there was no sign of service.
4. The seal hunting season started the seventh, and by the sixteenth some soap and water were very welcome.
5. A desire to sleep cut his eyes like scissors, but he continued to work and smoke because the last sentence had to be written by Saturday.

351-375

1. The Sunday school teacher told every student that those who suffer know the true meaning of the soul.
2. Sometimes a tailor will return a summer suit still soiled.
3. The soldier sat down to a supper which started with soup and ended with strong, sweet wine.
4. Every tenant was warned by telephone or telegram that he must sweep his side of the street.
5. When you subtract the price of the tax stamp, those stockings from the south cost something more than ours.

376-400

1. This is twice that my uncle has left his theater tickets in his other trousers.
2. They start to travel on the tenth or twelfth and return by the twentieth, a week before Thanksgiving.
3. Together we'll pick twelve men tomorrow, and thirteen more next Thursday.
4. Today the rain drove thirty thousand people toward the exit gates, with not one umbrella among them.
5. Billy tore his pants, but one touch of a thread to his mother's tongue and they were ready for a new trial.

Basic List Continued

ribbon
sail
sandwich
Santa Claus
Saturday
scissors
seal
season
sentence
September
service
seventeen
seventh
several
should
shoulder
sight
sign
silver
sister
sixteenth
sixth
sleep
smoke
soap

soldier
something
sometimes
soul
soup
south
stamp
still
stockings
street
strong
student
subtract
suffer
suit
summer
Sunday
supper
sweep
sweet
tailor
teacher
telegram
telephone
tenant

tenth
Thanksgiving
theater
thirteen
thirty
thousand
thread
Thursday
ticket
today
together
tomorrow
tongue
tore
touch
toward
travel
trial
trousers
twelfth
twelve
twentieth
twice
umbrella
uncle

401-425

1. The **visitor** can't **understand** how the **United States** is **governed until** he has seen **Washington.**
2. Without **warning**, a **wasp** stung the **wagon** driver who had gone for a **walk** to get some **water.**
3. By a **voice vote**, the group approved the idea to **watch** and **wait** for the results of the **wage** conference.
4. The **warm weather** was not **usual**, and the **vegetable** crop in the **village** would grow that much sooner.
5. While he will let you **weigh** him, he will not **welcome** any effort to **wake** him up to the need of a trim **waist.**

426-450

1. **Yesterday** that **young woman** became the **wife** of the owner of the **zinc** mine.
2. **Your** answer was **worth zero** because you described the **wrong zone.**
3. The **zoo** was proud of the **white fox, whose** arrival last **year** had created great **wonder.**
4. On his **winter** vacation he **woke** early every day to don his **yellow** skis and **zigzag** along the trails with the **zeal** of a boy.
5. Without a care in the **world,** he ate his dinner with great **zest,** and then looked out of his **window** as the plane began to **zoom** along at an ever faster rate.

Basic List Continued

understand
United States
until
usual
vegetable
village
visitor
voice
vote
wage
wagon
waist
wait
wake
walk
warm
warning
Washington
wasp
watch
water
weather
weigh
welcome
while

white
whose
wife
window
winter
without
woke
woman
wonder
world
worth
wrong
year
yellow
yesterday
young
your
zeal
zero
zest
zigzag
zinc
zone
zoo
zoom

Average List

Sentences
1-25

1. **According** to experts, an **actor** or **actress** must be born with **ability** and cannot **acquire** it.
2. **Afterward** I shall **accompany** you to the **affair** because it will be to your **advantage** to **accept** the award.
3. To go **abroad** sounded like good **advice**, but her **absence** would be an **admission** of the **actual** reason for leaving.
4. We **absolutely** cannot **acknowledge** your pass since the **addition** of secret work forces us to **abolish** former rules of **admittance**.
5. Those who **adopt** this country should develop an **accent** that people **admire**, and can **accomplish** this by attending schools that **advertise** courses in speech.

26-50

1. So **anxious** was he to work in the **airplane** factory that any **apartment** near it would **appear** to be **agreeable**.
2. Blind **ambition** refuses **allegiance** even to the **altar**, and will answer any **appeal** that feeds its **appetite** for power.
3. The **amendment** to the law forced each **agency** not to **approve** an **applicant** who was an **alien**.
4. Your **approach** to the **argument** would be of **amusement** to **anybody**, but does not **alter** the facts.
5. Tim sprained his **ankle** in the **agriculture** course and asked whether **anyone** would **arrange** to take his **arithmetic** homework to his next class.

51-75

1. The **arrival** of the **attorney** for the **association** caused a **battle** in the **assembly**.
2. I can **assure** you that no **attempt** will be made to **assist** you with the **baggage** until every **article** is checked.
3. With an **awful** scar on one cheek and a **bandage beneath** his eye, the **beggar** looked like a wounded **beast**.

Average List Continued

4. The price for the barrel is beyond what it was awhile ago and has become no bargain.
5. Many a backward glance was cast at the beefsteak party on the beach as the balance of the group left to cast its ballot.

Words

ability	agency	arrival
abolish	agreeable	article
abroad	agriculture	assembly
absence	airplane	assist
absolutely	alien	association
accent	allegiance	assure
accept	altar	attempt
accompany	alter	attorney
accomplish	ambition	awful
according	amendment	awhile
acknowledge	amusement	backward
acquire	ankle	baggage
actor	anxious	balance
actress	anybody	ballot
actual	anyone	bandage
addition	apartment	bargain
admire	appeal	barrel
admission	appear	battle
admittance	appetite	beach
adopt	applicant	beast
advantage	approach	become
advertise	approve	beefsteak
advice	argument	beggar
affair	arithmetic	beneath
afterward	arrange	beyond

Average List Continued

76-100

1. The **boarder** would beat his **breast** and **boast** that every day he read the **Bible** he kept in the hall closet.
2. You may **borrow** the **bicycle**, but don't try a **burst** of speed because the worn **brake** may earn you a **bruise**.
3. According to the **calendar**, the **cafeteria** today will serve corned beef, **cabbage**, and a **biscuit** as light as a cherry **blossom**.
4. With a **breath** of pride, Fenton recalled rising from **bootblack** to **blacksmith** to **candidate** for **bureau** chief.
5. He decided to **bury** the **bundle** of papers and the **cablegram** under the **bridge** and not **breathe** a word about them.

101-125

1. The **children** were ready to **celebrate** when told there was a **choice** between **cereal** and **chocolate**.
2. A **century** later, the letters of the **captain** were found in a small **carriage** left in the **cellar** of the **castle**.
3. He asked the **cashier** for **carfare** to the **capital** where he would get the **certificate** to be a **chauffeur**.
4. A **carpenter** was sent to the upper **chamber** to repair a damp **circle** in the **ceiling** near the **chimney**.
5. Since it was not in his **cheerful character** to **cheat** or turn to **charity** for help, he decided to sell his **cattle** instead.

126-150

1. To **conquer** the **climate** on the **coast**, **clothe** yourself in **comfortable** fashion.
2. Our **Constitution** states that only **Congress** can **consider** matters that **concern commerce**.
3. Good **citizenship** must **consist** of the desire to **complain** about any **condition** against the **common** good.

Average List Continued

4. After the **concert,** she took her **companion** to a little shop where they could sip a cup of **cocoa** in **complete comfort.**

5. The **complaint** about the new plan of the **college** to **connect** the various schools is that it will **commence** before anyone can **compare** it to the old program.

Bible	capital	citizenship
bicycle	captain	climate
biscuit	carfare	clothe
blacksmith	carpenter	coast
blossom	carriage	cocoa
boarder	cashier	college
boast	castle	comfort
bootblack	cattle	comfortable
borrow	ceiling	commence
brake	celebrate	commerce
breast	cellar	common
breath	century	companion
breathe	cereal	compare
bridge	certificate	complain
bruise	chamber	complaint
bundle	character	complete
bureau	charity	concern
burst	chauffeur	concert
bury	cheat	condition
cabbage	cheerful	Congress
cabinet	children	connect
cablegram	chimney	conquer
cafeteria	chocolate	consider
calendar	choice	consist
candidate	circle	Constitution

Average List Continued

151-175

1. During the **conversation**, he offered good **counsel** about the **contract**, but failed to **convince** us to **continue** with the work.
2. The **cottage** in the **country** will **contain** a long work **counter** with **copper** trim.
3. A **coward** considers his lack of **courage** in **dangerous** situations a **cruel curse**.
4. In the **course** of repairing the **damage** to the **dairy** plant, the **crew** found a **cradle** used in colonial days.
5. The **daily** market **curve** showed that the **custom curtain** business was not worth a **crumb**.

176-200

1. Unless you can **declare** war on the **delight** offered by **dessert**, you need not **describe** how you are going on a **diet**.
2. His **decision** to make a **declaration** that the **deal** had driven him into **debt** would **deceive** no one.
3. The **delegate** claimed that **defeat** faced **democracy** if we allowed economy to **destroy** our **defense** plans.
4. After the train had left the **depot**, the old **democrat** looked over the **deed** he had to **deliver** when he reached his **destination**.
5. I must **differ** with the **dictionary** because this **diamond** is a **descendant** of those used to **decorate** the royal crown.

201-225

1. As the **duke** paused on his way **downstairs**, he was at **ease** and looked like an **eagle** standing at the **edge** of a cliff.
2. If she did **discover** that the **domestic** was **dishonest**, she would have to **discuss** it with the **district** officer.
3. It was **difficult** to **discharge** the **director** because he was so **earnest** and **eager** to please.

Average List Continued

4. No **doubt** few would **disagree** that we had to **educate** every **druggist** in the new treatment of the **disease**.
5. In **due** time he began to **dream**, and it seemed that his **direct double** was coming in his **direction**.

contain	deal	difficult
continue	debt	direct
contract	deceive	direction
conversation	decision	director
convince	declaration	disagree
copper	declare	discharge
cottage	decorate	discover
counsel	deed	discuss
counter	defeat	disease
country	defense	dishonest
courage	delegate	district
course	delight	domestic
coward	deliver	double
cradle	democracy	doubt
crew	democrat	downstairs
cruel	depot	dream
crumb	descendant	druggist
curse	describe	due
curtain	dessert	duke
curve	destination	eager
custom	destroy	eagle
daily	diamond	earnest
dairy	dictionary	ease
damage	diet	edge
dangerous	differ	educate

Average List Continued

226-250

1. To avoid an **error**, **enclose** the **employment** slip in an **envelope**, and mail it to your **employer**.
2. The **engineer** seemed to **enjoy** his **effort** to make the **elevator** work by hand as well as by **electricity**.
3. **Everybody** was told to be **especially** careful to make an **exact** drawing of the **engine**, and to try not to use an **eraser**.
4. Before you **entertain**, try to **engage** someone to **embroider** the tablecloth to **establish** the **effect** of handmade linen.
5. After the **election**, he decided to **escape** to **Europe** to inspect the new **electric** plants of the British **Empire**.

251-275

1. In our **experience**, this is just an **excuse** to **exchange** the **faucet** at our **expense**.
2. It was an **extreme example** of a **female** hat, with a long **feather** and what seemed like a **feast** of fruits.
3. The **failure** of his appeal to the **federal** courts meant that the state would **execute** the **famous** prisoner without further **examination**.
4. Why doesn't the **examiner explain** to that **fellow** that he should become **familiar** with the **export** laws?
5. A **fault** of those who cannot **fasten** themselves to some **faith** is that they can give no **external expression** to their emotions.

276-300

1. The **foreman** of the **freight** department **found** it hard to resist **frequent** dishes of **fried** fish.
2. Unless you wear a **flannel** shirt, you will **freeze** during the **flight** because it may be your bad **fortune** to run into some **fierce** winds.

Average List Continued

3. On the **following** day the **funeral** was held for the lonely **figure** who had **frozen** to death near the **fountain**.
4. **Finally** the old **florist** came **forth** and asked the **feminine** customer to **forgive** him for being late.
5. A country built on a **firm foundation** of **freedom** tries to be **friendly**, but does not **frighten** easily if rejected.

effect	examination	feminine
effort	examiner	fierce
election	example	figure
electric	exchange	finally
electricity	excuse	firm
elevator	execute	flannel
embroider	expense	flight
empire	experience	florist
employer	explain	following
employment	export	foreman
enclose	expression	forgive
engage	external	forth
engine	extreme	fortune
engineer	failure	found
enjoy	faith	foundation
entertain	familiar	fountain
envelope	famous	freedom
eraser	fasten	freeze
error	faucet	freight
escape	fault	frequent
especially	feast	fried
establish	feather	friendly
Europe	federal	frighten
everybody	fellow	frozen
exact	female	funeral

Average List Continued
301-325

1. The garment found in the garage was covered with generous smears of grease and smelled of gasoline.
2. To furnish the art gallery with genuine old furniture is one of the first jobs the governor will assume.
3. With a gentle smile, the lady in the blue gown goes toward the door to greet the tall gentleman.
4. It was funny to see the goose looking at a geography book like a general making future plans over a map.
5. In great fury, Peters rushed out to see who had thrown garbage into the furnace, but the culprit was gone and further search was useless.

326-350

1. In the hygiene class we were told that hominy grits with honey could not keep one healthy, however much was eaten.
2. As he took the harness off the handsome horse, his hearty hello showed his happiness that the harvest was over.
3. The guard asked for the honor to guide the guest to the history classes.
4. So great were her honest grief and guilt that she seemed to be heading for a state that would affect her health.
5. From the height of his window he threw the pot handle in a hurry, hoping to convince the dog not to howl at the heaven above.

351-375

1. No immigrant need remain ignorant if he is industrious in his efforts to inquire and get information about his new land.
2. Industry and labor will hold an important meeting immediately and will include talk about an increase.
3. To show his independence, the industrial leader refused to imitate the idea because it would injure his name.

Average List Continued

4. We must stress the **importance** of confining certain **insane** types because **improvement** for them is **impossible** and they may cause **injury** to someone.

5. In its **innocence,** youth is **impatient** to be **independent,** and needs the **influence** of older heads to **illustrate** how harmful this can be.

funny	grief	idea
furnace	guard	ignorant
furnish	guest	illustrate
furniture	guide	imitate
further	guilt	immediately
fury	handle	immigrant
future	handsome	impatient
gallery	happiness	importance
garage	harness	important
garbage	harvest	impossible
garment	heading	improvement
gasoline	health	include
general	healthy	increase
generous	heaven	independence
gentle	height	independent
gentleman	hello	industrial
genuine	history	industrious
geography	hominy	industry
goes	honest	influence
gone	honey	information
goose	honor	injure
governor	however	injury
gown	howl	innocence
grease	hurry	inquire
greet	hygiene	insane

Average List Continued

376-400

1. An **invitation** was sent to the **agent** to collect the second **installment** on the **insurance** for the crown **jewel** of the **kingdom**.
2. By ordering the **inspector** to **investigate** the quality of the canned **juice**, the **judge** showed a fine sense of **justice**.
3. Let me **introduce** Mr. Kent, whose **intention** during the **interview** is to **interpret** the **judicial** report.
4. After putting some **kerosene** into a **kettle**, the **janitor**, following the **instruction** sheet, poured it on the **insect** nest.
5. Our **journey** to the **internal** region is to settle the **issue**, and remove the **jealousy** that has blown tempers as high as a **kite**.

401-425

1. To gain more **knowledge** for her **license** test as **librarian**, Sally attended every **lecture** at the **library**.
2. **Label** Tom a **liar**, if you will, but he said only some cheese on **lettuce** leaves and glasses of **lemonade** were served at the **lawn** party.
3. The **lawyer** told the **leader** of the **legion** that new **legislation** made him **liable** for the actions of his group.
4. Under the **lantern** was a sign on the **laundry** door knob, and I saw I was at **liberty** to sign a **lease** for the building.
5. Besides scratching her **knuckle**, the **kitten** had put such a **knot** in the wool on the **leather** chair that no one could **knit** with it now.

426-450

1. A **manual** of **material** needed to **manufacture** the new **locomotive** was issued with the **machinery**.
2. The slight **maiden** taking her **marriage** vows with her **masculine** partner made a **lovely** picture before the **magistrate**.
3. **Madam**, this luxury **mattress** is sewed by special **machine**, and is advertised in every leading **magazine**.

Average List Continued

4. It was **manifest** that the **lieutenant** could not **manage** his **liquor** since he acted as if he had been struck by **lightning**.

5. People with good **manners** would not **loiter** long at the **marble** staircase, for it was the **location** of the **liquid** refreshments.

insect	kitten	lieutenant
inspector	knit	lightning
installment	knob	liquid
instruction	knot	liquor
insurance	knowledge	location
intention	knuckle	locomotive
internal	label	loiter
interpret	lantern	lovely
interview	laundry	luxury
introduce	lawn	machine
investigate	lawyer	machinery
invitation	leader	madam
issue	lease	magazine
janitor	leather	magistrate
jealousy	lecture	maiden
jewel	legion	manage
journey	legislation	manifest
judge	lemonade	manners
judicial	lettuce	manual
juice	liable	manufacture
justice	liar	marble
kerosene	liberty	marriage
kettle	librarian	masculine
kingdom	library	material
kite	license	mattress

Average List Continued

451-475

1. In his **message** to the group, the **minister** had to **mention** the **mortgage** on the **modest** church property.
2. The **mistress** of the **millinery** shop had made a **model** in the **modern** **mode**.
3. **Minus** the **mosquito** bites, the **midnight** walk in the **meadow** would have left a wonderful memory.
4. With a **mighty** swing of his arm, the **miller** struck the **mechanic**, and soon every **merchant** on the street was watching the **mortal** combat.
5. A **messenger** was sent by the **military** governor of **Mexico** to ask for supplies of **molasses** and **mineral** spirits.

476-500

1. It seems to be in the **nature** of the **Negro** to have a **natural** sense of **musical** **movement**.
2. People of every **nationality** pass through the **narrow** entrance to New York harbor to escape the **neglect** of their **native** lands and seek **naturalization** here.
3. Her **neighbor** removed the **napkin** from the **mutton** stew and, seeing that **mold** had set in, said **nobody** should eat it.
4. The **naughty** boy was **mute** when the **neuter** gender was mentioned, and the teacher grabbed him by the **necktie** with **murder** in her eye.
5. Knowing the **nomination** would not come from a **neutral** source, if he came late, Collins strained **nearly** every **muscle** to start the **motor**.

501-525

1. Please **notify** the **oculist** that I shall **obey** his request to come to his **office** as soon as I get **official** leave.
2. The **odor** of cooked **oatmeal** and an **onion** being fried in **olive** oil assailed his **nostril**.

Average List Continued

3. There was **objection** to the **occupation** of the **northern** lands, and he dared not **offend** public **opinion**.

4. The **nurse** took an **oath** before a **notary** that it would be her **obligation** to meet all rules with **obedience**.

5. It did not **occur** to him that it would be a **nuisance** to **occupy** the center of the boat until he had to **oblige** by taking an **oar**.

meadow	mosquito	northern
mechanic	motor	nostril
memory	movement	notary
mention	murder	notify
merchant	muscle	nuisance
message	musical	nurse
messenger	mute	oar
Mexico	mutton	oath
midnight	napkin	oatmeal
mighty	narrow	obedience
military	nationality	obey
miller	native	objection
millinery	natural	obligation
mineral	naturalization	oblige
minister	nature	occupation
minus	naughty	occupy
mistress	nearly	occur
mode	necktie	oculist
model	neglect	odor
modern	Negro	offend
modest	neighbor	office
molasses	neuter	official
mold	neutral	olive
mortal	nobody	onion
mortgage	nomination	opinion

Average List Continued

526-550

1. One **patron** in **particular** was ready to **oppose** the new **orchestra** unless it included an **organ**.
2. The city **ordinance** stated that the **penalty** for a **peddler** who bothered a **patient** would be the **payment** of a fine.
3. When he felt the **package** slipping out of his **palm**, he turned **pale** because neither **parent** would **pardon** him if he broke the vase.
4. He thought it **peculiar** that the **passport** of the **passenger** **opposite** him in the **parlor** car was being checked.
5. Unless your **partner** has booked **passage** on a fast boat, it will be an **otherwise** **ordinary** task to **overtake** him.

551-575

1. A **pleasant** moment at the **picnic** was the playing of a **popular** **piano** piece on the **phonograph**.
2. The **police** asked the **physician** to test the amount of **poison** put into the **pepper** eaten by the **porter**.
3. After the **poll**, every **plumber** in the union gave a **pledge** of ten **per cent** of his wages for the **political** drive.
4. It was a **pleasure** to sit on the **porch** with a **pitcher** of lemonade before us, and have a **polite** talk on **politics**.
5. Temple refused to **perform** at his own **peril** unless a **photograph** were taken of a **portion** of the **plaster** wall that looked ready to fall out.

576-600

1. The **priest** was unable to **prevail** upon the **prince** to allow a **prayer** to be said for the **prisoner**.
2. It is **probable** that the department will **proclaim** new **postal** rates to **preserve** the **present** services.
3. If you **prefer** to **prepare** the mixture by the old **process**, **pour** some **powder** into a cup and then add water.

Average List Continued

4. Send **postage**, and we will solve your **problem** of how to **practice** the dance **position** in **private**.
5. He had to **pretend** to be able to **produce** any results because he was eager to **procure** the **praise** of the **powerful** men.

oppose	pepper	position
opposite	per cent	postage
orchestra	perform	postal
ordinance	peril	pour
ordinary	phonograph	powder
organ	photograph	powerful
otherwise	physician	practice
overtake	piano	praise
package	picnic	prayer
pale	pitcher	prefer
palm	plaster	prepare
pardon	pleasant	present
parent	pleasure	preserve
parlor	pledge	pretend
particular	plumber	prevail
partner	poison	priest
passage	police	prince
passenger	polite	prisoner
passport	political	private
patient	politics	probable
patron	poll	problem
payment	popular	process
peculiar	porch	proclaim
peddler	porter	procure
penalty	portion	produce

Average List Continued
601-625

1. I propose that we serve prune pudding and pumpkin pie at the end of the program.

2. The professor agreed to promote the pupil when he would prove he could pronounce each word.

3. Every property deed had a purple stamp which the owner had to purchase as proof that a proper deal had been made.

4. To protect the public, the city will prohibit the sale of the product for a profit, and will punish offenders.

5. The purpose the legal profession had in wanting to publish the report was to provide a prompt answer to its critics.

626-650

1. With her quantity of raven hair, the queen was easy to recognize as she entered the railroad coach.

2. His refusal to quarrel about the rake showed that he was trying to redeem himself and forget his former record as a rebel.

3. On a recent radio program, a rabbi was asked to recite some prayers that had been found in an old reader.

4. She found a piece of rabbit fur of good quality in her purse, and thought it queer that she couldn't recall whose it was.

5. During the recess, Joe was really quite happy when he was offered some of the raisin cake that was lying on the kitchen range.

651-675

1. The reporter asked Father Crowley to relate how he had brought religion to that remote region.

2. A special drive was on to request every regular Republican voter who was a resident to register for the election.

3. It was a relief to learn that Summers, who was held in high regard, would be able to represent the republic even under the new regulation.

Average List Continued

4. In moments of **repose**, people can **repent** their sins, **repair** their souls, **regain** their confidence, and **renew** their hope.

5. You must **resist** any desire to **repeat** your **reference** to the incident at the **resort**, even to a **relative**.

product	purse	reference
profession	quality	regain
professor	quantity	regard
profit	quarrel	region
program	queen	register
prohibit	queer	regular
promote	quite	regulation
prompt	rabbi	relate
pronounce	rabbit	relative
proof	radio	relief
proper	railroad	religion
property	raisin	remote
propose	rake	renew
protect	range	repair
prove	raven	repeat
provide	reader	repent
prune	really	reporter
publish	rebel	repose
pudding	recall	represent
pumpkin	recent	republic
punish	recess	republican
pupil	recite	request
purchase	recognize	resident
purple	record	resist
purpose	redeem	resort

Average List Continued

676-700

1. When the **retail** trade took a **rude** drop, the **salesman** knew it would be hard to **restore** his old salary.
2. A platter of **roast** beef, a green **salad**, and a piece of **rye** bread caused the **sailor** to **salute** his host.
3. Hit by a **rough** blow with the **rubber** hose, the **robber** let out a **roar** and fell into the **rubbish** heap.
4. Before I **resume** my talk, I **respectfully** ask my **rival** to **reveal** why his firm sold **rotten** fruit to the hospitals.
5. **Review** the **sacrifice** it took to check the **revolt**, and you can see why this man must **retain** your **respect**.

701-725

1. In his **search** to **secure** a good **secretary**, he will **select** only one who is **serious** about her work.
2. The **servant** brought some **sausage** and eggs to the **senator**, and a **shallow** **saucer** of milk for his pet cat.
3. A **scream** had been heard at the **scene**, but evidence was **scarce** since everyone had been able to **scatter** before the police could **seize** a witness.
4. Since we want the **screen** over the **sewer** openings now, don't **scratch** your head like a **scholar** but get your **share** of the work done.
5. You may have to **settle** some **severe** differences of opinion before your **selection** for the post will **satisfy** the **senate**.

726-750

1. Even the **shawl** gave little **shelter**, and when a **slight** **shiver** was followed by a **sneeze** she went inside.
2. It is **simple** to **sharpen** the tool so that a **single** turn will cut a **smooth** **slice**.
3. **Somebody** must have given a **signal** to the **sheriff** who has just **shown** his **shield** and taken charge.

Average List Continued

4. The **society** members were **sincere** when they said that his **signature** on the letter of resignation was a **source of sorrow** to them.
5. Kicking off a **slipper**, she watched the **soda** clerk in **sober silence** as he tried to **shovel** some ice cream into a plate.

respect	satisfy	sharpen
respectfully	saucer	shawl
restore	sausage	shelter
resume	scarce	sheriff
retail	scatter	shield
retain	scene	shiver
reveal	scholar	shovel
review	scratch	shown
revolt	scream	signal
rival	screen	signature
roar	search	silence
roast	secretary	simple
robber	secure	sincere
rotten	seize	single
rough	select	slice
rubber	selection	slight
rubbish	senate	slipper
rude	senator	smooth
rye	serious	sneeze
sacrifice	servant	sober
sailor	settle	society
salad	severe	soda
salary	sewer	somebody
salesman	shallow	sorrow
salute	share	source

Average List Continued

751-775

1. As the old **statesman** rose on the **stage** to give his **speech,** we sang "The Star-Spangled Banner" with great **spirit.**
2. The retired **station** agent would sit in the town **square** and **spread** crumbs of **stale** bread for his **sparrow** friends.
3. At the **steam** table, I found the choice to be **steak, spinach** and corn, or **spare** ribs in a **special** sauce.
4. When the **speaker** made a **statement** about those who **sponge** on the state and **steal** public funds, some **spice** came into his talk.
5. A **splendid** appeal by the chairman broke the **steady** effort of the **standard** bearers of the **southern** group to form a **splinter** party.

776-800

1. All of a **sudden,** a shell ripped through a **steel** plate in the **stern** near the **steerage** and caused a **stir** in the engine room.
2. **Strife** had broken out above the **stream** where only **superior** land **strength** would **succeed** in turning back the enemy.
3. He tried to **stretch** his arm, but the **strange** pain in his **stomach** made it a **struggle** to **steer.**
4. By a **stroke** of luck, the **substitute** for the regular **stenographer** was such a **success** that Miss Webb had no need to **summon** help.
5. A **stripe** is in **style** this year, but we **suggest** that you **submit** a few more sketches on the **subject.**

Average List Continued

southern

spangle

spare

sparrow

speaker

special

speech

spice

spinach

spirit

splendid

splinter

sponge

spread

square

stage

stale

standard

statement

statesman

station

steady

steak

steal

steam

steel

steer

steerage

stenographer

stern

stir

stomach

strange

stream

strength

stretch

strife

stripe

stroke

struggle

style

subject

submit

substitute

succeed

success

sudden

suggest

summon

superior

Average List Continued

801-825

1. To see the actor **swallow** the **sword** was a **surprise** to the **surgeon** who was once heard to **swear** it was impossible to do.

2. The **supply** company had a **terrible** trip through the **swamp** since one **swarm** of insects after another rose from its **surface**.

3. On a **tablet** in the old **temple**, someone with **talent** had outlined the **system** of worship under the **supreme** ruler.

4. If you want the **support** of the chief **teller**, don't lose your **temper** if he refuses to **telegraph** the money to the **sweater** concern.

5. I **suppose** it wasn't odd in the summer to see a man sitting in front of a **tenement**, **suspenders** down, shirt **tail** out, and **sweat** pouring from his brow.

826-850

1. The **tiger** has been a **thorn** in the sides of the people of that **territory**, and has struck **terror** in the hearts of the **timid**.

2. A distant clap of **thunder** seemed to **threaten** rain, which we **thought** would relieve the **thirst** of the crops **throughout** the area.

3. Shot in the **thigh**, the **thief** tried to escape by the **toilet** window, but met with **total** defeat when he slipped on a **thimble** and fell.

4. A little **tomato** juice, a piece of **toast**, and a pipeful of **tobacco** were enough of a **tonic** to **tide** him over until supper.

5. Pointing with his **thumb** toward the **tidy** little house, he spoke of a **token** deposit before **title**, and **therefore** asked for a check.

Average List Continued

supply	territory
support	terror
suppose	therefore
supreme	thief
surface	thigh
surgeon	thimble
surprise	thirst
suspenders	thorn
swallow	thought
swamp	threaten
swarm	throughout
swear	thumb
sweat	thunder
sweater	tide
sword	tidy
system	tiger
tablet	timid
tail	title
talent	toast
telegraph	tobacco
teller	toilet
temper	token
temple	tomato
tenement	tonic
terrible	total

Average List Continued

851-875

1. A trailer truck had hit a trolley, and police were unable to clear up traffic in the tunnel for an hour.
2. The tribe had sent the trustee a copy of an original native tune as a tribute to his good treatment of them.
3. If you twist some plastic twine around that ugly tube, you can use it as a towel bar.
4. Since no trace of the typist could be found, the treasurer went to the typewriter and pounded out the transfer of funds report.
5. On his return from a tough treasure hunt, the traveler ate the turkey gladly, but refused the cooked turnip.

876-900

1. Not knowing it was unlawful to unbutton his uniform, the unfortunate cadet was caught and sent upstairs.
2. Although a bit unusual, the university will undertake to unite the union members by offering a course in labor problems.
3. The urge to be useful is a universal trait, and people are unhappy if old age or illness makes them feel useless.
4. For some unknown reason, a boy climbed upward to an unfurnished room in the upper story, and was unseen by us.
5. Unlike his unhealthy brother, Jim will find the uneven, untried climate harmless, unless we are mistaken.

Average List Continued

tough	unbutton
towel	undertake
trace	uneven
traffic	unfortunate
trailer	unfurnished
transfer	unhappy
traveler	unhealthy
treasure	uniform
treasurer	union
treatment	unite
tribe	universal
tribute	university
trolley	unknown
trustee	unlawful
tube	unless
tune	unlike
tunnel	unseen
turkey	untried
turnip	unusual
twine	upper
twist	upstairs
typewriter	upward
typist	urge
ugly	useful
unable	useless

Average List Continued

901-925

1. The **usher** tried in **vain** to reach the **vacant** seat, but to his **utter** disgust the small man was the **victor** in the race.
2. **Veto** that bill and you will **vex** everyone in the **valley** who will consider it a **victory** for the forces of **vice**.
3. On her **vacation** she loved to walk in the **vale** where a **variety** of **valuable** orchids were everywhere in **view**.
4. **Various** meats, including **veal**, were cooking in the **utensil**, whose great **value** was its **vapor** seal.
5. Every **vein** of the captain of the **vessel** stood out as he tried his **utmost** to **verify** the report that he had been the **victim** of a plot.

926-950

1. So **weak** had the **voyage** made the **weary** girl that all she could do was **wail** and **weep**.
2. He showed a **visible** **wealth** of talent with the **violin**, and it would be a **waste** not to make playing it his **vocation**.
3. The **waiter** had put such a **volume** of **vinegar** in the dish that the **vile** taste made the diner **vomit**.
4. At the **wedding** of the **wealthy** broker, a **watchman** was hired to keep the grounds **void** of intruders who might **wander** in.
5. With a look of **virtue** on his face, the **warden** announced with **vigor** that he had found the **weapon** in a **violet** bed.

Average List Continued

usher	vigor
utensil	vile
utmost	vinegar
utter	violet
vacant	violin
vacation	virtue
vain	visible
vale	vocation
valley	void
valuable	volume
value	vomit
vapor	voyage
variety	wail
various	waiter
veal	wander
vein	warden
verify	waste
vessel	watchman
veto	weak
vex	wealth
vice	wealthy
victim	weapon
victor	weary
victory	wedding
view	weep

Average List Continued

951-975

1. We heard the **witness whisper** to the **widow** that he would **withdraw** from the case if she were **willing**.
2. **Wheat** was sent by the **western** world **wherever** and **whenever** it could serve the **welfare** of the poor.
3. **Whatever** the **wholesale** price of the **wheelbarrow** is, be sure to get the proper **width** and a rubber **wheel**.
4. **Whence** the **wine** barrel had come was beyond his **wisdom**, but the **weight** of it made him pause to **wipe** his **brow**.
5. The **whistle** of the boy coming down from the **willow** tree stopped short when the **wicked** old farmer struck him with a **wire whip**.

976-1000

1. The **youth** became a **worker** for the **Zion** movement because he wanted **worse** than ever to end the **woe** his people had suffered.
2. He did no more than **wrench** his **wrist**, but his main **worry** was how to **worm** his way out of this **wreck**.
3. His career reached the **zenith** when his **wonderful** carving of a **wooden zebra** was judged **worthy** of the grand prize.
4. I wouldn't mind if **yonder wretch** would only **yawn** when I play the **zither**, but the **worst** of it is he snores, too.
5. Trying to take the **yeast** stain out of her **woolen wrap**, all she did was **wound** herself on the **zipper**.

Average List Continued

weight	woe
welfare	wonderful
western	wooden
whatever	woolen
wheat	worker
wheel	worm
wheelbarrow	worry
whence	worse
whenever	worst
wherever	worthy
whip	wound
whisper	wrap
whistle	wreck
wholesale	wrench
wicked	wretch
widow	wrist
width	yawn
willing	yeast
willow	yonder
wine	youth
wipe	zebra
wire	zenith
wisdom	Zion
withdraw	zipper
witness	zither

Advanced List

Ninety Day Trial
Sentences

1-20

1. A **capacity** crowd watched the **American** team win the **benefit** basketball game.
2. With the **cooperation** of the salesman, who showed her the **catalog**, she was able to buy some **acceptable clothes**.
3. Much **criticism** was directed against the **committee** for using its **authority** without a legal **basis**.
4. No one in good **conscience** would issue a **bulletin** without first trying to **ascertain** the **bearing** it would have on the case.
5. Your **courtesy** in offering to **accommodate** my **acquaintance** will be **cordially** repaid.

21-40

1. A **guardian** will be **duly** named to keep **definite** control over financial matters.
2. By some **miracle**, the **exhausted** boys reached the **dormitory** before their **mischief** was discovered.
3. In the **judgment** of the dealer, it would be an **excellent edition** to add to his collection of classic **literature**.
4. The chief **executive** of the **government** made an **extraordinary farewell** address.
5. We will not **interrupt** the building of the **extension** if we can **determine** the **existence** of a proper permit.

41-60

1. **Undoubtedly** the **monarchy** would not return since a **recommendation** had been made to exile the **sovereign**.

Advanced List Continued

2. It will be **necessary** for me to get a **quantity** of slides to meet a **requirement** of the **zoology** class.
3. I heard one **peasant murmur** that the **warrant** for the arrest of the official should contain a **treason** charge.
4. Have the good **sense** on this **occasion** to take a **thorough** grasp of the **opportunity**.
5. Our **original** plan was to sign for a **partial** period **prior** to any **permanent** arrangement.

Ninety Day Trial
Words

acceptable	definite	monarchy
accommodate	determine	murmur
acquaintance	dormitory	necessary
American	duly	occasion
ascertain	edition	opportunity
authority	excellent	original
basis	executive	partial
basketball	exhausted	peasant
bearing	existence	permanent
benefit	extension	prior
bulletin	extraordinary	quantity
capacity	farewell	recommendation
catalog	financial	requirement
clothes	government	sense
committee	guardian	sovereign
conscience	interrupt	thorough
cooperation	judgment	treason
cordially	literature	undoubtedly
courtesy	miracle	warrant
criticism	mischief	zoology

Advanced List Continued
Sentences
1-25

1. Accordingly, we will adjourn this case until you bring a signed affidavit from your accountant that the agreement existed.
2. No adjective could describe his agony as he knelt in the aisle to ask the Almighty for an abatement of his sorrow.
3. An abundance of alcohol always would affect him with an air of abandon and gay adventure.
4. The acknowledgment that use of the alloy would be all right and in accordance with plans was accidentally mislaid.
5. Man will not accustom himself to letting others abridge his freedom, however much they seek to achieve his admiration by speaking affectionately of justice.

26-50

1. When the altos joined in the ancient song, our appreciation mounted because the chorus sounded altogether like a group of angels.
2. Apparently, the ambassador had sought the arrangement of an appropriation for his area.
3. From the appearance of things, the operation for appendicitis could not be performed on the arctic explorer because no antiseptic was anywhere to be found.
4. The ambitious architect was glad to announce that his apparatus had been approved for the annual show.
5. Approximately a dozen tutors had tried vainly from every angle to get Roger to appreciate his ancestors, but he remained aloof.

Advanced List Continued

Words

abandon

abatement

abridge

abundance

accidentally

accordance

accordingly

accountant

accustom

achieve

acknowledgment

adjective

adjourn

admiration

adventure

affect

affectionately

affidavit

agony

agreement

aisle

alcohol

alloy

all right

Almighty

aloof

altogether

altos

ambassador

ambitious

ancestors

ancient

angels

angle

announce

annual

antiseptic

anywhere

apparatus

apparently

appearance

appendicitis

appreciate

appreciation

appropriation

approximately

architect

arctic

area

armory

Advanced List Continued

51-75

1. A large **audience** came to the **balcony** of the **armory** to watch the **banquet** being given for the star **athlete**.
2. On the **average**, he kept ten sacks of **barley available** in his **basement** for the **assistance** of the poor.
3. I shall **assign** an **attendant** to tell the **author** not to **ascend** the platform before the people **assemble** and are seated.
4. You can **assume** it would **astonish** him to learn of the **barbarous** treatment even **babies** were given after the village was **attacked**.
5. Her **beauty** could so **attract** men that they were forever **attaching** themselves, although she kept **assuring** them they would go **bankrupt** buying her presents.

76-100

1. On her **blouse** she wore two **cameos** which had **bronze** clips and **butterfly** designs in **brilliant** colors.
2. The **burglar** did not **beware** the dog at the **boundary** of the estate, but one **bestial** growl sent him up the **bough** of a tree.
3. In the **beginning** it was our **belief** that the **bricklayer** had gone over our **budget** by a hair's **breadth**.
4. Who would **boycott** a party where **besides** sandwiches there was a cool **beverage bubbling** in a large **bucket**?
5. At the **burial**, someone **brought** a **bugle** to his lips, as the captain, holding the **bridle** of his horse, stood with head bowed under his **burden** of grief.

Advanced List Continued

arrangement
ascend
assemble
assign
assistance
assume
assuring
astonish
athlete
attaching
attacked
attendant
attract
audience
author
available
average
babies
balcony
bankrupt
banquet
barbarous
barley
basement
beauty

beginning
belief
besides
bestial
beverage
beware
blouse
bough
boundary
boycott
breadth
bricklayer
bridle
brilliant
bronze
brought
bubbling
bucket
budget
bugle
burden
burglar
burial
butterfly
cameos

Advanced List Continued

101-125

1. The **ceremony** was in **celebration** of the end of the **campaign** which had carried the **champion** to the peak of his **career**.
2. **Canoeing** down the river, Tom pulled his **camera** out of its **canvas** cover so that he could **capture** the lovely sight of the distant **cathedral**.
3. When the **cargoes** arrived at the **cannery**, the **celery** and **cauliflower** crates were unloaded, but the **cantaloupe** shipment was sent back.
4. As the **cavalry** swept past the **cemetery** toward the **captive** company, the roar of the **cannon** did not **cease**.
5. From its office in the **capitol**, the **census** bureau announced a new **canvass** of the **changeable** population if **capable** workers could be found.

126-150

1. In the **chapel**, the **community choir** sang several **Christian** hymns in **commendable** fashion.
2. By **comparison**, the **cobbler** could **claim** more **chargeable** accounts than the **clothier**.
3. The **commission** sent a **circular** through the **colony**, warning that **chauvinism** had always been a threat to **civilization**.
4. According to the report of the **chemist**, someone with **coarse chestnut** hair has **committed** the crime against the **colonist**.
5. A **communication** from the **circus** manager said that under no **circumstances** would the **combination** dive be permitted from the top of the **column**.

Advanced List Continued

camera
campaign
cannery
cannon
canoeing
cantaloupe
canvas
canvass
capable
capitol
captive
capture
career
cargoes
cathedral
cauliflower
cavalry
cease
celebration
celery
cemetery
census
ceremony
champion
changeable

chapel
chargeable
chauvinism
chemist
chestnut
choir
Christian
circular
circumstance
circus
civilization
claim
clothier
coarse
cobbler
colonist
colony
column
combination
commendable
commission
committed
communication
community
comparison

Advanced List Continued

151-175

1. **Confidence** in his **compass** made him **completely** sure he would avoid **confusion** even if he went a **considerable** way into the woods.
2. If **neither** side will **concede** ground in the matter of **compensation,** you will **compel** me to **conclude** the conference.
3. He had to **confess** that he had cheated in the class **competition,** and it was small **consolation** that his **comrade** did not **condemn** him.
4. **Consequently,** after the **compilation** of the facts, everyone could **comprehend** why an effort was made to **conceal** their **connection** with the senator.
5. Although he would try to **construct** a new **composition** for the **complexion** cream, he was **conscious** of the consequence of failure.

176-200

1. At the **convention,** one doctor told how he had **created** a **continuous** check on the **contagious** disease by setting up a **controlled** group.
2. In a **contemptible** effort to avoid **criminal** charges, the **corrupt controller** of the **corporation** left town.
3. Several **countries** on the **continent** organized a **council** in order to **consult** with one another about the proper **conveyance** of defense plans.
4. Only the **continual** sound of a **cricket** disturbed the strange **creature** as he scrawled a bit of **correspondence** with a large **crayon.**
5. **Contrary** to our expectations, the **contractor** had shown a **cordial** interest in our **convenience** by making the porch **convertible** to an all year room.

Advanced List Continued

compass
compel
compensation
competition
compilation
completely
complexion
composition
comprehend
comrade
conceal
concede
conclude
condemn
conference
confess
confidence
confusion
connection
conscious
consequence
consequently
considerable
consolation
construct

consult
contagious
contemptible
continent
continual
continuous
contractor
contrary
controlled
controller
convenience
convention
convertible
conveyance
cordial
corporation
correspondence
corrupt
council
countries
crayon
creation
creature
cricket
criminal

Advanced List Continued
201-225

1. The delicate care with which the nurse placed a cushion behind the cripple seemed to be a denial of her reputation for cruelty.
2. These dahlia seeds will give delightful flowers, and if you cultivate the cucumber patch you will have a delicious addition to your summer menu.
3. It was curious to see how the decrease of supplies in the cupboard had made her dependent on the delivery service.
4. In his deposition before the judge, Mr. Cole pointed out the degree to which the once dependable market had fallen into a current decline.
5. A cursory glance at the dense growth made him decide to defy the decree of his landscaper not to use the grass cutter.

226-250

1. From the description of the footprints, the detective believed that the difference in depth between the two was destined to solve the case.
2. He would derive more benefit if he were to deprive himself rather than devour everything in sight and have difficulty later trying to digest the food.
3. The dilemma he faced was the need to devote full time to the development of a new design for the stamping device.
4. In the directory was the address of her despised relative, but dignity would not allow one to descend so low as to visit the disagreeable man.
5. Diphtheria in this desolate area would bring destruction and despair unless desperate efforts were made to fight it.

Advanced List Continued

cripple
cruelty
cucumber
cultivate
cupboard
curious
current
cursory
cushion
cutter
dahlia
decline
decrease
decree
defy
degree
delicate
delicious
delightful
delivery
denial
dense
dependable
dependent
deposition

deprive
depth
derive
descend
description
design
desolate
despair
desperate
despised
destined
destruction
detective
development
device
devote
devour
difference
difficulty
digest
dignity
dilemma
diphtheria
directory
disagreeable

Advanced List Continued

251-275

1. Her **distress** did not **disturb** those who could **distinguish** real pain and **dismiss** this as a mood that would soon **disappear**.
2. I must say I am **disappointed** at your **discontent**, and I **disapprove** your **distinct** effort to **discourage** the others.
3. To **disobey** would be **disastrous**, but there was no way to **dissolve** the **dispute** without meeting with his **displeasure**.
4. We can **dispose** of the goods on **display**, although it's a **disgrace** to sell such **divine** dresses so low, even at a **discount**.
5. A **discovery** was made in the **dispensary** that certain **distinctive** markings helped remove the **disguise** from the odd skin **disorder**.

276-300

1. From his **duffel** bag he took the plan which showed how the **electronic** system would **duplicate** colors without need of **dyeing** the **elegant** cloth.
2. Hardly had the **echoes** of her **doubtful** past faded from the **divorce** trial when the **dreadful** news arrived that she had **drowned** herself.
3. The **educator** called the attention of the **editor** to the **doctrine** that an unstable **economy** will create **division** among the people.
4. When the **draftsman** **edited** the report of the **electrician**, he suggested an **elementary** way to make the estimate **divisible** into a unit price.
5. Nothing short of an **earthquake** will move **drowsy donkeys**, and it **doesn't** seem strange that sometimes their drivers would be **elated** if one came along.

Advanced List Continued

disappear
disappointed
disapprove
disastrous
discontent
discount
discourage
discovery
disgrace
disguise
dismiss
disobey
disorder
dispensary
display
displeasure
dispose
dispute
dissolve
distinct
distinctive
distinguish
distress
disturb
divine

divisible
division
divorce
doctrine
doesn't
donkeys
doubtful
draftsman
dreadful
drowned
drowsy
duffel
duplicate
dyeing
earthquake
echoes
economy
edited
editor
educator
elated
electrician
electronic
elegant
elementary

Advanced List Continued

301-325

1. Your rescue of the leader from his encounter with the enormous elephant will entitle you to his eternal thanks.
2. Having lost the esteem of the emperor, Tito would now have to emigrate elsewhere, but he was not equipped for travel.
3. It was not easy for the engraver to estimate the cost of enlarging the emblem because of the erasure in the plan.
4. Billy would embrace the chance to run an errand, especially since mother would soon encourage him to supply entertainment for the guests on the piano.
5. In the emergency, one employee turned his energy upon the equipment in a loyal endeavor to repair it before too much time was lost.

326-350

1. Everyone was exhausted by the excess of weeping at the news that Carlos had been exiled and would be expatriated for ten years.
2. One explanation of the failure of the exclusive fashion everywhere was its exorbitant price.
3. Evidence that the trip was over would exhilarate the faithful members of the expedition, and make them cry out in exultation.
4. The exhibit would allow no exception, and if he dared exceed the limits of design he would expose himself to being expelled.
5. To exclaim about a threat of famine would excite the people and cause them to explore why other lands should excel theirs.

Advanced List Continued

elephant
elsewhere
emblem
embrace
emergency
emigrate
emperor
employee
encounter
encourage
endeavor
energy
engraver
enlarging
enormous
entertainment
entitle
equipment
equipped
erasure
errand
especially
esteem
estimate
eternal

everyone
everywhere
evidence
exceed
excel
exception
excess
excite
exclaim
exclusive
exhausted
exhibit
exhilarate
exile
exorbitant
expatriated
expedition
expelled
explanation
explore
expose
exultation
faithful
famine
fashion

Advanced List Continued

351-375

1. A slight **flutter** of his **feeble** hand showed that the **forcible** feeding was having a **favorable** effect on what had seemed a **fatal** illness.

2. Our **foremost** regret was that we had to **forsake** this **fertile** land where fruits of wonderful **flavor** could **flourish** all year.

3. A **feature** of the **festival** was the showing of a film of the **fiery** singer who was the **favorite** actress in the south.

4. It would not be **feasible** to market the **fluid fertilizer** unless they were **fortunate** in getting someone to **finance** the project.

5. **Fidelity** is a **fixture** in marriage and tends to **forge** happiness for all but the **frivolous** who **flatter** themselves on being different.

376-400

1. At first the **furrier** would **frown,** and then become **furious** at his **futility** in learning **grammar.**

2. The **glitter** in the **gorgeous** hair of the **gracious** actress made her look like a **glorious goddess.**

3. To **fulfill** his promise to rid the grounds of every **grass-hopper,** the **gardener** made **gradual** use of a **fuel** oil spray.

4. He was **fully** prepared to swear it was the **gospel** truth that he had seen a **ghost** wearing **goggles galloping** by on a horse.

5. Every **generation** in the family seemed to **graduate** a **glazier** who was a **genius** at creating **graceful** figures in blown **glass.**

Advanced List Continued

fatal
favorable
favorite
feasible
feature
feeble
fertile
fertilizer
festival
fidelity
fiery
film
finance
fixture
flatter
flavor
flourish
fluid
flutter
forcible
foremost
forge
forsake
fortunate
frivolous

frown
fuel
fulfill
fully
furious
furrier
futility
gallop
gardener
generation
genius
ghost
glazier
glitter
glorious
goddess
goggles
gorgeous
gospel
graceful
gracious
gradual
graduate
grammar
grasshopper

Advanced List Continued

401-425

1. The youthful **heir** was **grateful** for the way his **haughty guardian** was **handling** the affairs of the estate.
2. **Hereafter,** before I buy a tool to check the **growth** of the hedge, the **hardware** store will have to **guarantee** it.
3. Paul felt **guilty** about his **hatred** for the greedy old man and could **hardly** allow him to lie helpless in the **gutter.**
4. While I may **groan** about it, I **hereby** give you my word that **henceforth** I shall **heartily** welcome the work at the **gymnasium.**
5. Don't **grieve** over the lack of **harmony** but **hasten** to show your **gratitude** that at least the main **grievance** has been removed.

426-450

1. **Hurrah** for the **humble hoe** which destroys the **immunity heretofore** enjoyed by the weed.
2. **Herewith** is an example of how this **idol** of the **household** listeners **appeals** to the **illiterate** who cannot see his **hypocrisy.**
3. In deep, **hollow** tones the organ poured forth the **immortal hymn** of man's **heroic** struggle against the **horrible** forces of evil.
4. Anything blocking the **horizon** is a **hindrance** on a highway and should be removed **immediately** before it produces the **horror** of a crash.
5. Your **ignorance** about animals is beyond **imagination,** but come **hither,** and I shall tell you all about this **immense hippopotamus.**

Advanced List Continued

heretofore

herewith

heroic

highway

hindrance

hippopotamus

hither

hoe

hollow

horizon

horrible

horror

household

humble

hurrah

hymn

hypocrisy

idol

ignorance

illiterate

imagination

immediately

immense

immortal

immunity

grateful

gratitude

greedy

grievance

grieve

groan

growth

guarantee

guardian

guilty

gutter

gymnasium

handling

hardly

hardware

harmony

hasten

hatred

haughty

heartily

hedge

heir

henceforth

hereafter

hereby

Advanced List Continued

451-475

1. The infinite faith every inhabitant had in the imperial ruler's wisdom seemed to indicate that no one could induce them to revolt.
2. If you dare impose an inferior instrument on the artist, you will not only inconvenience him but arouse his indignation.
3. My initial impression of that individual served only to inspire an instant dislike for him.
4. At his inauguration he spoke with intelligence of an indivisible nation, and attacked by innuendo those who would undermine every institution held dear by us.
5. Further inquiry showed that this was one instance where one could inherit a tendency that would incline him toward indigestion.

476-500

1. In league with the old knight, Fenton worked out an invention which made invisible all signals sent across the isthmus.
2. The legislature made it a crime for any jeweler to sell without an invoice, and whether he could justify it was deemed irrelevant.
3. In the interior of her handbag was discovered the intimate little ivory figure which the laundress had found irresistible.
4. A poorly labeled bottle of iodine will not kindle much laughter in a laboratory.
5. Irregular jewelry purchases by the jockey forced the board to intercede and turn him over to the jurisdiction of the courts.

Advanced List Continued

imperial
impose
impression
inauguration
incline
inconvenience
indicate
indigestion
indignation
individual
indivisible
induce
inferior
infinite
inhabitant
inherit
initial
innuendo
inquiry
inspire
instance
instant
institution
instrument
intelligence

intercede
interior
intimate
invention
invisible
invoice
iodine
irregular
irrelevant
irresistible
isthmus
ivory
jeweler
jewelry
jockey
jurisdiction
justify
kindle
knight
labeled
laboratory
laughter
laundress
league
legislature

Advanced List Continued

501-525

1. **Maybe mama** wanted a **manicure** because she wished to look like the **majority** when she went for her **literacy** test.
2. The lonely, **majestic** figure walked up the **macadam** road toward the **magnificent mausoleum**.
3. Keep this **lively** book on your **mantel** since it is good reading and can **likewise lighten** your **leisure** moments.
4. Her **Majesty** found the **mansion** so **lonesome** that she would **loose** a wail like a caged **lunatic** whenever she was left by herself.
5. In the **meantime** he learned that even a **mature** man would have to be built like a **longshoreman** to **maintain** the **lodge** all year.

526-550

1. By her new **method**, the **medium** could with a **mere** wave of her hand **mesmerize** anyone who gave her even **moderate** attention.
2. When the child had the **misfortune** to contract the **measles**, the **midwife** became **miserable** and lost all signs of **mirth**.
3. His **misery** mounted when he saw in the **mirror** that the **mischievous** driver had fixed the **meter** to record extra **mileage**.
4. A **memorandum** regarding the **melon** shipment pointed out that the **merchandise** had a **mixture** of quality and did not meet **minimum** standards.
5. **Meanwhile**, as the sad **melody** was played, he stood **midst** the crowd, wishing to **mingle** with those who had come to the **memorial** services.

Advanced List Continued

leisure
lighten
likewise
literacy
lively
lodge
lonely
lonesome
longshoreman
loose
lunatic
macadam
magnificent
maintain
majestic
majes v
majority
mama
manicure
mansion
mantel
mature
mausoleum
maybe
meantime

meanwhile
measles
medium
melody
melon
memorandum
memorial
merchandise
mere
mesmerize
meter
method
midst
midwife
mileage
mingle
minimum
mirror
mirth
mischievous
miserable
misery
misfortune
mixture
moderate

Advanced List Continued

551-575

1. By **mutual** consent, the **musician** and his wife decided to move out of the **neighborhood** because the **moist** climate was lowering their **morale**.
2. Although the body of the **monarch** may **molder** beneath his **monument**, the **narrative** of his deeds will live forever in the hearts of the **multitude**.
3. How the **monkeys** had escaped from the **municipal museum** would always remain a **mystery** to the motor-cycle officers assigned to catch them.
4. **Moreover**, his **motive** in wishing to make us **nervous** by talking about a **mysterious monster** was not clear.
5. **Nevertheless**, the **moral** of the story is that **moisture** in tobacco will no more reduce **nicotine** than sugar will sweeten **mustard**.

576-600

1. **Numerous** members of the **organization** came to the **palace** for the **occurrence**, but **pandemonium** broke loose when the king failed to appear.
2. He had **originally** made the **observation** that to **ordain** a minister in an **opera** house was **outrageous**, and most people agreed.
3. **Obedient** though the **orphan** was, he had to offer **opposition** against the effort to **oppress** him for every minor **offense**.
4. It was a **novelty** for us to **observe** how the **oyster** would **occasionally nourish** itself.
5. To **operate** that **orchard** of **ours** allowed time for only an **occasional** trip to buy some clothing or an **ornament** for the house.

Advanced List Continued

moist

moisture

molder

monarch

monkeys

monster

monument

moral

morale

moreover

motive

motorcycle

multitude

municipal

museum

musician

mustard

mutual

mysterious

mystery

narrative

neighborhood

nervous

nevertheless

nicotine

nourish

novelty

numerous

obedient

observation

observe

occasional

occasionally

occurrence

offense

opera

operate

opposition

oppress

orchard

ordain

organization

originally

ornament

orphan

ours

outrageous

oyster

palace

pandemonium

Advanced List Continued

601-625

1. **Papa** was **partial** to **peanut** butter in his **pastry**, but in neither of the **pantries** could we find any.
2. People lining the **pavement** could **perceive** the look of the true **patriot** on the faces of the **parachute** troops who were passing in **parade**.
3. Every **paragraph** of the speech he delivered with such **passion** before **parliament** seemed like a **pearl** of wisdom dropped from **paradise**.
4. A good **percentage** of the horses stood **parallel** to each other in the **peaceful pasture**, looking as if they had been retired on **pension**.
5. His **patience** was rewarded when the **patent** office approved his **pattern** for a **penicillin** extractor, and returned it by **parcel post**.

626-650

1. The great **persistence** a **pigeon** shows when it travels miles from its **perch** and returns is no **phenomenon** because I have **personally** seen it done.
2. No **phrase** in the **petition** demanded **perfection**, but it sought to **persuade** the governor to grant **permission** for action to be taken.
3. As he leaned against a **pillar** near the **piazza** and breathed the **perfume** of the flowers, a **pistol** shot **pierced** the air.
4. Before the **picnicking** began we thought we would **perish** from **perspiration**, but some **pineapple** juice followed by sandwiches and a **pickle** salad soon revived us.
5. Because his religious **philosophy** was not **permissible** at home, the **pilgrim** became a **pioneer** in search of **perpetual** freedom.

Advanced List Continued

pantries
papa
parachute
parade
paradise
paragraph
parallel
parcel post
parliament
partial
passion
pastry
pasture
patent
patience
patriot
pattern
pavement
peaceful
peanut
pearl
penicillin
pension
perceive
percentage

perch
perfection
perfume
perish
permissible
permission
perpetual
persistence
personally
perspiration
persuade
petition
phenomenon
philosophy
phrase
piazza
pickle
picnicking
pierced
pigeon
pilgrim
pillar
pineapple
pioneer
pistol

Advanced List Continued

651-675

1. One **premise** of modern **poetry** is that such common things as **potatoes** or **poultry** can become proper subjects for a poem.
2. **Preach** all he might about the value to **posterity** of the **preamble** to the Constitution, the **politician** still offered no policy we could understand.
3. She was **practically** mad about the **precious pottery** of the ancient **potentate,** and showed her **preference** by outbidding everybody.
4. A **plunge** from the **platform** was no answer to her **poverty,** even though she had lost every **possession** to a convicted **polygamist.**
5. One should not **precede** the other, but public education and **practical** measures will prevent the **possibility** of a **pneumonia plague.**

676-700

1. Since I'm no **prophet,** I shall not **presume** to **prophesy** what **progress** you will make, but what I **prescribe** should help.
2. **Prominent** people considered it a **privilege** to lend their **presence** to the **procession** in honor of the **princess.**
3. **Probably** the old **principle** will be applied, and no one will **preside** over a **primary** election who has not had **previous** training.
4. The **proprietor,** a **prey** to wild schemes before, said there was no **prospect** he would accept this **proposition** without study and **preparation.**
5. Not to **prolong** his talk, the **principal** concluded with the **prophecy** that a large **proportion** of the graduates would **proceed** to college and do well.

Advanced List Continued

plague

platform

plunge

pneumonia

poem

poetry

policy

politician

polygamist

possession

possibility

posterity

potatoes

potentate

pottery

poultry

poverty

practical

practically

preach

preamble

precede

precious

preference

premise

preparation

prescribe

presence

preside

presume

previous

prey

primary

princess

principal

principle

privilege

probably

proceed

procession

progress

prolong

prominent

prophecy

prophesy

prophet

proportion

proposition

proprietor

prospect

Advanced List Continued

701-725

1. There is no **question** that the **publication** will **qualify** for a higher **rating** when it makes **provision** for wider news coverage.

2. Every **reasonable** plan had been tried, and now only **Providence** would bring **prosperity readily** to the **realm**.

3. It was no **puzzle** why the people in the upper **province** did not **protest** over the **quarantine** because they had to **realize** it was for their own good.

4. **Psychology** tells us that **punishment** will not **quench** a strong spirit, but will merely **provoke** it to **pursue** its course all the harder.

5. The **prosperous** farmer enjoyed life, and a **rainbow** or blue sky could **quicken** his **pulse** at the sheer **rapture** of the colors.

726-750

1. In his **replies**, the **representative** said he **regretted** that to **relieve** the situation there would have to be a **referendum**.

2. As no **remittance** of a **receipt** was made in my **remembrance**, we'll place the **remainder** of the balance in the accounts **receivable**.

3. To **recede** before public opinion meant to **reject** his ideals, and no man of **renown** could **renounce** his beliefs nor take **refuge** in fear.

4. If you **reflect** on what **remedy** will give you **release**, you will find that **religious** faith may **reconcile** you to your troubles.

5. Let us **rejoice** in the **reign** of this **remarkable** king who allows no **repetition** of the evils we had to **reckon** with before.

Advanced List Continued

prosperity	recede
prosperous	receipt
protest	receivable
Providence	reckon
province	reconcile
provision	referendum
provoke	reflect
psychology	refuge
publication	regretted
pulse	reign
punishment	reject
pursue	rejoice
puzzle	release
qualify	relieve
quarantine	religious
quench	remainder
question	remarkable
quicken	remedy
rainbow	remembrance
rapture	remittance
rating	renounce
readily	renown
realize	repetition
realm	replies
reasonable	representative

Advanced List Continued

751-775

1. To **rescue** Carver was quite a **responsibility** because Gorman, **revolver** in hand, stood on a **ridge** and could easily **riddle** anyone who came near.

2. **Respective** doctors had told His **Reverence** that the pain seemed to **resemble rheumatism,** but he thought the idea **ridiculous.**

3. His **reputation** forced him to **resign** rather than **reverse** himself and **retreat** from a position he considered beyond **reproach.**

4. Since the decision of the **revenue** agent to tax your **reserve** fund is not **reversible,** thoughts of **revenge** will not **resolve** your difficulty.

5. Pancho **reveled** in the **restless** spirit of **resistance** that no one could **restrain** from becoming **revolutionary** in action.

776-800

1. We tried to be **sanitary,** but containers were **scarce** and we had to **rinse** out **salmon** or **sardine** cans and use them.

2. If the **rumor** that he had sold his **scheme** to the enemy were true, it would **ruin** the **scientist** and might cause a **riot.**

3. It must give that **rooster satisfaction** to keep his **schedule** because he will **rouse** us at dawn even on the Sabbath.

4. To call his **salve** a **sample** of the **sacred** ointment was bad enough, but to make it **salable** was **sacrilegious.**

5. On his **route** to the ranch, Chambers found a **savage** wild horse that took all his **science** to **saddle** in **satisfactory** fashion.

Advanced List Continued

reproach

reputation

rescue

resemble

reserve

resign

resistance

resolve

respective

responsibility

restless

restrain

retreat

reveled

revenge

revenue

reverence

reverse

reversible

revolutionary

revolver

rheumatism

riddle

ridge

ridiculous

rinse

riot

rooster

rouse

route

ruin

rumor

Sabbath

sacred

sacrilegious

saddle

salable

salmon

salve

sample

sanitary

sardine

satisfaction

satisfactory

savage

scarce

schedule

scheme

science

scientist

Advanced List Continued

801-825

1. A **sedative** and short rest on the **sofa** calmed the **seamstress** who had let out a **shriek** when the gas flame began **singeing** her hair.
2. Last **semester**, at the **settlement** house, a **socialist** delivered a **series** of talks on subjects in which he **sincerely** believed.
3. With a **sigh**, Mr. Walton agreed with his friend, **Sergeant** Peters, that the painting **situated** in the **social** hall would have to be freshly **shellacked**.
4. The **shrewd** salesman was so **skillful** he could convince the most **sensible** that the **site** for their home was **similar** to the best.
5. All the **shepherd** did was **snatch** a pair of **shears** and cut the **slippery serpent** in two.

826-850

1. With a **solemn** nod, Mr. Ford revived Sally's **spirits** when he **specified** he would use enough **starch** to make her dresses **sparkle**.
2. We watched Mr. Gates **stalk** about the **stable** and **stare** at every corner because the **squirrel** was still **somewhere** around.
3. The **splendor** of a **spectacle** involving twenty **stately sopranos** singing together could **stagger** the imagination.
4. To **solve** the problem, he would tie every **solitary squash** to a **stake** and then **sprinkle** each with the insect powder.
5. Her **stationary** work and daily **solitude** made the **sphere** of interest of the old **spinner somewhat** limited.

Advanced List Continued

seamstress	solemn
sedative	solitary
semester	solitude
sensible	solve
sergeant	somewhat
series	somewhere
serpent	sopranos
settlement	sparkle
shears	specified
shellacked	spectacle
shepherd	sphere
shrewd	spinner
shriek	spirits
sigh	splendor
similar	sprinkle
sincerely	squash
singeing	squirrel
site	stable
situated	stagger
skillful	stake
slippery	stalk
snatch	starch
social	stare
socialist	stately
sofa	stationary

Advanced List Continued

851-875

1. Although **successful** in stealing **stationery** from the **studios,** he was too **stupid** to see he was **subtly** being given rope to hang himself.

2. The **substance** of the speech by the **superintendent** was that he would **strengthen** the **strict** application of the **statute** against smoking.

3. **Sulphur** fumes caused him to **stumble** on his way up the **steeple,** but his **stubborn** will was **sufficient** to keep him from falling.

4. Her **sullen** reaction to the **suggestion** by the **supervisor** to **stitch** the new pattern carefully was **suitable** reason for her dismissal.

5. As we passed the **strait,** the crew had to **subdue** a stowaway who had tried to force the cook to **surrender** a jar of **strawberry** jam.

876-900

1. When **testimony** revealed that the **switchman** could not have been near the **tavern,** the **surrogate** showed some **sympathy** and resumed reading the will.

2. The orders were to **surround** the tannery where the **teamster** worked and to hide in a **thicket** until the **suspect** came out.

3. **Symmetry** in design was no **temporary symbol** to the **textile** firms, but a permanent reminder that this would **sustain** their business.

4. To **tease** the **thirsty** boys, Sis poured some **syrup** into a glass and added milk, **thereby** making them mad with **temptation.**

5. When we **surveyed** the **temperature** on the **thermometer,** we realized that even in the **temperate** zone an occasional **tempest** was possible.

Advanced List Continued

stationery	surrogate
statute	surround
steeple	surveyed
stitch	suspect
stowaway	sustain
strait	switchman
strawberry	symbol
strengthen	symmetry
strict	sympathy
stubborn	syrup
studios	tannery
stumble	tavern
stupid	teamster
subdue	tease
substance	temperate
subtly	temperature
successful	tempest
sufficient	temporary
suggestion	temptation
suitable	testimony
sullen	textile
sulphur	thereby
superintendent	thermometer
supervisor	thicket
surrender	thirsty

Advanced List Continued
901-925

1. In the **tragedy** of Caesar, we read how he returned in **triumph** and was **thrice** offered the **throne** by the Roman **throng**.
2. Whenever the **trumpet** announced a new **tributary** in the parade, it seemed to **torture** the **traitor** Cassius and make him **tremble** with rage.
3. Mr. Brice contracted **tonsillitis** trying to arrange **transportation** for every **trifle** contributed to swell the **treasury** of the **tuberculosis** fund.
4. We could **translate** the **twinkle** in the baron's eye as meaning he would forget the **tradition** of no **trespassing** on this lovely June **twilight**.
5. His **type** loved to **torment** others, and he would even **tread** on a **turtle** and **trample** it for the pleasure it gave him.

926-950

1. People would **vanish** into a secret **vault** under a **veil** of secrecy if they excited the **vengeance** of the old **tyrant**.
2. **Unfortunately**, in trying to keep the **ukulele underneath** the **umbrella**, Don dropped his **valise**.
3. **Ventilate** the room well because children **usually** regard the need to **vaccinate** them as **unnecessary tyranny** and are likely to faint.
4. His lack of **vanity** made him **uncertain** about how **usable** his **verse** would be, but it turned out to have **unexpected** merit.
5. When we did **venture** into the room, we found the **upholsterer**, almost **unconscious**, sitting **upright** on a pile of **velvet**.

Advanced List Continued

thrice	tyranny
throne	tyrant
throng	ukulele
tonsillitis	umbrella
torment	uncertain
torture	unconscious
tradition	underneath
tragedy	unexpected
traitor	unfortunately
trample	unnecessary
translate	upholsterer
transportation	upright
tread	usable
treasury	usually
tremble	vaccinate
trespassing	valise
tributary	vanish
trifle	vanity
triumph	vault
trumpet	veil
tuberculosis	velvet
turtle	vengeance
twilight	ventilate
twinkle	venture
type	verse

Advanced List Continued

951-975

1. The **victorious warrior** used a trick **whereby** he was able to **whirl** the **villain** over his head and cast him down to defeat.
2. **Wherefore** such a **vulgar** display of **violence** arose over a slight **violation** was the ground **wherein** our complaint was lodged.
3. Far from the **wholesome** outer world, the **witch** retired into the **wilderness whither** she could **worship** her evil spirits.
4. **Whoever** sees **womenfolk weave** cloth in poor light should warn them of the **weakness** of **vision** that may result.
5. **Whew**, letting that part of the tube **wither** away is **voluntary** on your part, but I would **vulcanize** it with some **virgin** rubber.

976-990

1. Nothing could **wrinkle** the **worsted** which was as soft as a spring **zephyr**.
2. So great was his **wrath** that the **wretched** boy would not **yield** though badly beaten.
3. The **Zulu** chief placed a **wreath** like a **yoke** around my neck.
4. As a relief from his **zoological** studies, Terry took a piece of **zwieback** and went over to play the **xylophone**.
5. If you believe in signs of the **zodiac**, those **zinnia** plants of **yours** will do well this year.

Advanced List Continued

victorious	wilderness
villain	witch
violation	wither
violence	womenfolk
virgin	worship
vision	worsted
voluntary	wrath
vulcanize	wreath
vulgar	wretched
warrior	wrinkle
weakness	xylophone
weave	yield
whereby	yoke
wherefore	yours
wherein	zephyr
whew	zinnia
whirl	zodiac
whither	zoological
whoever	Zulu
wholesome	zwieback

INDEX

Private Spelling List

_____

_____

_____

_____

_____

_____

_____

_____

_____

_____

_____

_____

_____

_____

_____

_____

Private Spelling List

_____

_____

_____

_____

_____

_____

_____

_____

_____

_____

_____

_____

_____

_____

Private Spelling List

THESE SYMBOLS GUARANTEE
THE BEST IN READING

POCKET BOOKS, INC. is the largest publisher of books in the world today in terms of the number of copies it has sold and is currently selling. Nearly 500,000,000 copies have carried the symbol of "Gertrude," the little kangaroo which is the colophon of POCKET BOOKS, INC., or the perky bird which is the trademark of CARDINAL EDITIONS, books of exceptional merit and value, priced at 25¢, 35¢ and 50¢.

Only genuine POCKET BOOK and CARDINAL editions carry these symbols. The titles are carefully chosen from the lists of all leading publishers and present the most distinguished and most widely diversified group offered today by any publisher of paper-bound books. Watch for these symbols. They are your guarantee of the best in reading at the lowest possible price.